D0319989

A NEW FINANCIAL DAWN:
THE RISE OF ISLAMIC FINANCE

A NEW
FINANCIAL DAWN

THE RISE OF
ISLAMIC FINANCE

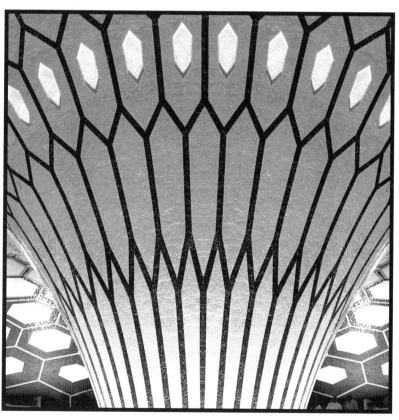

JOSEPH DIVANNA & ANTOINE SREIH
FOREWORD BY MICHAEL AINLEY

© Joseph A. DiVanna and Antoine Sreih 2009

All rights reserved. No part of this publication may be reproduced or transmitted in any form or by any means without prior written permission of the publisher.

The rights of Joseph A. DiVanna and Antoine Sreih to be identified as the authors of this work have been asserted in accordance with the Copyright, Designs and Patents Act 1988

Published in the United Kingdom
By Leonardo and Francis Press Ltd
Suite 41
23 King Street
Cambridge, CB1 1AH
Tel: +44 (0) 1223 693426
www.leonardoandfrancis.com

First published 2009

Printed in Great Britain by the MPG Books Group,
Bodmin and King's Lynn

Typesetting and editing by
Aardvark Editorial Limited, Norfolk

Cover design by Gabriel Research & Management – London
Graphics support by Head-e Design

ISBN-13: 978–1–905687–10–7   Paperback
ISBN-10: 1–905687–10–9   Paperback
ISBN-13: 978–1–905687–09–1   Hardback
ISBN-10: 1–905687–09–5   Hardback

A catalogue record for this book is available from the British Library

A catalog record for this book is available from the Library of Congress

CONTENTS

LIST OF FIGURES

LIST OF TABLES

FOREWORD

Over the last decade, Islamic banking has been a growing force in the international financial system but it remains something of a mystery to many conventional bankers. This book is both timely and relevant in giving a clear explanation of the underlying concepts and values, current practices and future opportunities. There is no doubt that the knowledge gap is holding the industry back and the authors bring out very well the continuing need for educating the markets and consumers.

The authors are farsighted but also realistic. They do not gloss over the real obstacles to moving the industry forward. In the UK, as elsewhere, there is a lack of liquidity in primary and secondary markets, a shortage of banking skills and trained Shariah scholars as well as conflicting interpretations of Shariah law. The recent progress towards resolving these issues is encouraging and it will need to continue if a new dawn for Islamic banking is to materialize soon.

Understandably, the key focus is on how Islamic banking can make the difficult transition from niche player to becoming an integral part of the global system. The main opportunities for expansion are analysed thoroughly, in particular among non-Muslims attracted by the industry's ethical base and in emerging markets where a very large part of the population has no access to banking products in any form. Taking advantage of these opportunities is the key question and initiatives in targeted marketing, improved quality of services and greater use of technology are rightly seen as a way forward. It will also be important for the industry to learn from the experience and ideas of their conventional counterparts and from each other. This book provides a useful framework for doing this.

MICHAEL AINLEY
Head of Wholesale Banks & Investment Firms Dept
Financial Services Authority

INTRODUCTION

At the time of the writing of this book, the global capital markets and their associated banking institutions are experiencing a collapse in value due to an overwhelming loss of confidence by consumers, investors and businesses. The credit crisis has eroded market confidence and reduced the appetite for risk to only the most fearless of investors in global markets. However, as traditional financial markets continue to falter, Islamic finance appears to be weathering the financial storm. Although Islamic finance is not immune, its fundamental structure is being tested in other ways, such as the continual problem of market liquidity.

Luis Maronese, the director of group corporate communications at Ithmaar Banking Group, has stated that 'the Islamic banking and finance model, which is heavily focused on fair risk sharing and emphasizes equity risk, has built-in stabilizers'.[1] Similar stabilizers do not underpin the conventional banking system. In the conventional system, the recent crisis has left bank stocks, which have traditionally been stable, slow-growing stalwarts of the markets, increasingly volatile, losing 50–90% of their value in a very short time. Conventional market dynamics have taken a new meaning, as previous indicators of a bank's performance have been jettisoned in favour of irrational reactions to disassociated information on potential threats to corporate performance. US and European markets have moved from investor to speculator based, as short-termism, with a continued focus on a one quarter ahead mentality, rules the day. Against this trend has been the steadfast rise of Islamic finance, which has seen a 27.8% rise in Shariah-compliant bank assets from US$500.4bn in 2007[2] to US$639bn in 2008.[3]

Although it would be tempting to add to the speculations on the root causes of the US-led banking and economic collapse, this book examines the current economic crisis in the context of how western markets influence Islamic financial innovation. In addition, we also briefly discuss how these market conditions are creating a fertile seedbed for the next generation of innovation in Shariah-compliant financial services. We will also review the similarities and differences in Islamic finance with conventional banking and finance counterparts in an effort to discover best practices in innovation. Our review then turns to the early results from Shariah-compliant banks at the vanguard of new product development. Understanding these new products and the behaviours and attitudes of customers using them is key to avert any missteps during the next generation of the Islamic finance markets' development. What has become evident is that one aspect of innovation in conventional banking over the past 20 years has led to the creation of complex financial products, which in turn has acted to destabilize and disrupt industrialized economies.[4] That said, understanding the successes and failures in conventional banks and their service offerings to customers is a vital component in developing a clear understanding of the role that Shariah-compliant financial institutions play in providing varying degrees of stability in national economies.

A Return to the Fundamentals

One key tool that conventional banks use in facilitating economic growth within a nation state is the dispensing of credit. The extension of credit in all its various forms is what facilitates modern economic activities for businesses and consumers. Without a steady flow of credit, national economies stagnate, decline or collapse.

The Latin root of the word credit is *credere*, which means to trust, similar to the Arab word *amanah*. Within a nation state, trust in the financial system is an implicit bond that provides citizens with a sense of stability and optimism. When social trust is compromised, the result is consumer pessimism and fear – credit is restricted and spending is curtailed. It is because of the unique nature of how banks act to provide implicit trust within a nation that governments treat banks substantially differently from other industries. For example, within a nation state, if a car manufacturer releases a bad or overpriced product, consumers respond by not purchasing the cars. Subsequently, the car company experiences financial distress and unless drastic action is taken, it will go out of business. The net result is one less car manufacturer operating in the nation and a loss of jobs. By contrast, in the financial markets, when a bank displays signs of distress, people panic, rushing to withdraw their savings, effectively making a bad situation worse for the bank. In the UK, this is exactly what happened in 2007, when Northern Rock collapsed. Historically, when consumers believe that one bank has failed, they rationalize that all banks are on the verge of collapse, which in turn feeds the panic.

Social Financial Cohesion

Financial institutions provide a nation with something not found in other industries, namely "social financial cohesion". Financial services are the "glue" that holds a nation's economy together by facilitating the commercial needs of business and making possible the wide variety of lifestyles enjoyed by consumers within a nation. Although this is an oversimplification of what is indeed a complex relationship between financial service providers, governments and consumers, it nevertheless provides an insight into why, during 2008, the US government elected to bail out banks and rejected appeals from US car manufacturers for similar measures. Interestingly, in 2009, President Obama finally decided to bail out General Motors due to the impact that the loss of jobs would have on the economy. The case of General Motors, however, is to be regarded as an exception.

In the context of Islamic finance, facilitating social financial cohesion is one of the main tenets in the operation of Shariah-compliant banks. It is because banks provide social financial cohesion that governments act to preserve banks during times of insolvency, and regulators move to keep the markets functioning. One could argue that during 2008, the actions taken by central banks to boost liquidity and support the markets had less to do with supporting individual financial institutions and more to do with boosting the level of confidence in world markets. Although one rarely thinks about trust as an element of the value proposition of a financial institution, it is clear that, without trust, a bank cannot facilitate the economic activities of businesses and consumers. Trust cannot be purchased, manufactured or fabricated – it must be earned.

Naturally, trust between a bank and a customer is a two-way process: the banker must demonstrate trust and customers must be trustworthy. When customers distrust banks, there is a flight towards the preservation of cash and economy. This is frequently the case in emerging markets, where the use of cash is preferred. In mature markets, when a bank loses customer trust, there is an exodus of customers to other banks. On the other hand, when banks distrust customers, credit is tightened, as banks alter the criteria for lending in order to systematically eliminate customers who are potential defaulters. Finally, if customers are indeed not trustworthy, they default on their obligations, which is, one could argue, one of the root causes of the subprime lending crisis in the USA.

To understand the role of trust in Islamic finance, the evolution of the industry and the need for innovation in the next generation of Shariah-compliant products, our discussion must venture briefly into an examination of the current global financial crisis. Although there are numerous theories accounting for what triggered the credit crisis and the underlying causes for economic instability in developed markets, for our purposes, we will focus on the issues of trust and social financial cohesion.

Fundamentally, the credit crisis in the USA has three market actors: creditors (banks and other lenders), regulators (market referees and rule makers) and borrowers (consumers and businesses). The vast majority of the press coverage surrounding the crisis has focused on the role of the first group, namely the banks as creditors and their laxity in credit policies over the past 20 years. Few stories discuss how the actions of banks were predicated on a continual need to meet shareholder expectations of growth and profit. For the sake of brevity, let us agree that the role the banks played was a catalyst for the crisis.

The second group of market actors portrayed by the media are the regulators who oversee market activities by establishing the boundaries of banking behaviour within a nation state. Their role in the crisis has yet to be fully understood. As regulators, they create the rules that govern banks' actions, and define what activities might violate the public trust. Consumers form the third group of actors; media coverage on the role of consumers as the originators or triggers of the crisis is rather more scarce, although consumers were, by all accounts, the reactants in the catalyst that perpetrated the crisis when they demonstrated their inability to repay loans. In the media search for the guilty party to be blamed for the crisis, perhaps we are overlooking the true culprits, namely consumers and their behaviours of living beyond their means and greed. An oversimplification of the credit crisis is that bankers misplaced their trust in subprime customers and customers misplaced their trust in bankers to provide them with financial acumen. One could argue that banks and customers naively misplaced their trust in governments' ability to monitor and regulate the situation. As a result, in early 2009, market confidence and public trust in most banking systems across the developed economies have severely decreased.

Once signs of a breach of trust occurred, bankers – remembering that shareholders are often ill-tempered and will sell shares on the smallest item of bad news – moved unilaterally to tighten credit by establishing increasingly stringent criteria for lending. One thing that sets the current economic crisis apart from historical market crashes is the unprecedented amount of cross-border financial product interoperation. In the summer of 2007, the US credit crisis hit Europe as the French insurer AXA and the German bank IKB saw devaluations in funds that were exposed to risks in the US markets, while BNP Paribas froze the Parvest Dynamic Fund, Euribor Fund and Eonia Fund as the market for mortgage-backed securities imploded.[5] As the crisis continued, the US market witnessed the collapse of

Bear Stearns, the government takeover of Fannie Mae and Freddie Mac, and the disintegration of Lehman Brothers. In 2008, the markets saw the semi-nationalization of banks across the world, including venerable banks such as Citigroup, Lloyds TSB, Royal Bank of Scotland, Halifax and many others. The shear enormity of the crisis may never be fully understood as market watchers fear that the US$800bn banking bailout is the beginning of a more serious problem. Let us be clear on the role of perceived trust; in the case of Bear Stearns, for example, its collapse was not a product of insolvency. Rather, other market players feared that as market pressure increased, they could no longer place their trust in the company. One could argue that a simple lack of confidence was the undoing of Lehman Brothers.

Consumers and businesses in any given society inherently trust banks as the neutral third party to facilitate transactions between two parties. In the past, the word 'trust' was sometimes incorporated into the name of the financial institution, such as Manufacturers Hanover Trust (USA) or the Overseas Trust Bank (Hong Kong). Even today, banks still use the word trust in their names and brand identities, such as First Trust Bank (UK), Cayman National Bank & Trust Company (Cayman Islands) and The Trust Bank (Ghana). Although banks rarely market themselves with slogans like "trust us" or "you can place your deposits and trust in us", their brand identities reflect a perception of an implied trust. Historically, trust in a bank's brand identity was straightforwardly represented by heavy stainless steel bank vault doors that were often within view of customers, tall marble columns outside the front door representing strength, and bars on the windows to imply impregnability. The image of a bank was to portray a sense of trust that customers' deposits were secure. For an illustration of how trust has played such a large role in perpetuating confidence in a nation's financial system, we can cite a historically recent example. To reinforce the ideal of trust in the US market after the collapse of the financial markets in 1929, the Federal Deposit Insurance Corporation (FDIC) was created from the Glass-Steagall Act of 1933 to guarantee the safety of deposits. In the later part of the twentieth century, the imagery of vaults and columns was replaced by skyscrapers and other symbols of power to provide customers with a sense of confidence that a big bank was safe and unable to fail.

Trust in Muslim Communities

Just as trust plays an integral role in providing social financial cohesion in non-Muslim societies, Shariah-based finance fills the same role in Islamic communities. Shariah-based finance provides the economic glue that enables society to function by facilitating commerce in much the same fashion as its conventional counterparts. What is different in Islamic finance and conventional finance is an explicit versus an implicit trust. In conventional banking markets, there is an implied trust between an institution and the customer, represented by images of power, size of institution and number of customers. In Islamic finance, trust is explicit, declared by both the institution and the customer as the role played by the institution is that of an impartial facilitator of financial transactions. Therefore, trust in a Shariah-compliant institution is paramount for it to achieve its objectives, facilitate the lifestyles of customers and to serve the greater needs of society.

As trust in conventional markets continues to erode, Islamic finance as an industry is rapidly evolving into a viable alternative to conventional sources and forms of capital for Muslim and non-Muslim business. To describe Islamic finance as simply a system of finance that happens to be devoid of interest understates the true nature of the Islamic ideal, namely the fair and equitable exchange between two parties. Islamic finance is the execution of a financial transaction through a trusted third party that acts to balance risk and return between parties. Corporations such as Tesco (UK) and Toyota (Japan) have used Islamic financial instruments to meet their capital requirements.

The New Dawn

It is with this understanding of the role of Islamic finance in global communities that we examine how innovation is being embraced by the industry in the development of the next generation of products. In Chapter 1, The Evolution of Islamic Finance, we review a short history of Islamic finance, placing the new forms of Islamic-based financial product innovation into the context of an industry transitioning between revolution and evolution. It is our intention to illustrate that the fundamentals of Shariah principles transcend a universal set of ideals shared between Muslims and other faiths. The moral and ethical constructs of Shariah appeal to an individual's basic desire for fairness and equality. From this fundamental knowledge of Shariah principles, we agree that the interpretive nature of Shariah lends itself to an implicit ability to be applied in many ways, thus creating a seedbed for financial innovation.

Our discussion in Chapter 2, Innovation and Market Growth, centres on understanding the implications of new product development on the variations in market maturity. Not all markets for Islamic finance are at a high level of customer maturity – instead, they range from the growing sophistication in the UK, Malaysia and Middle Eastern markets to the less complex markets within emerging nations such as Pakistan, Indonesia and Kenya. Several nations have started to develop markets in specialized Islamic finance products where they are maturing at vastly different rates. A corollary discussion focuses on the growing level of product sophistication as institutions move away from the typical conventional product mix towards more "de novo" products. In addition, our analysis of the markets looks at how Islamic institutions are expanding their offerings up and down the economic pyramid, across lifestyle and cultural divides, devising offerings that appeal to Muslims and non-Muslims alike. To place these issues in the context of how these factors influence Islamic financial institutions, we briefly examine the impact of the evolution of markets and products on the internal disciplines within institutions as they engage a multidimensional growth agenda.

Chapter 3, Emerging Financial Hubs, considers the emergence of transnational financial centres (or hubs) in several cities, including Abu Dhabi, Doha, Dubai, Kuala Lumpur, Kuwait City, London, Paris, Manama and Riyadh, as financial gateways to Muslim populations across the globe. Our exploration into the next generation of Islamic finance reviews the specialization in financial products, such as *sukuk*, *takaful* and other financial instruments, as a foundation for these emerging centres of Islamic finance to interoperate with each other, perhaps as a new model of global finance.

Our debate in Chapter 4, New Forms of Capital for Twenty-first-century Business, centres our attention on the emerging forms of Shariah-compliant capital for twenty-first-century business. As new financial instruments emerge, businesses, both Muslim and conventional, need to have an in-depth understanding of how to use Islamic financing as a viable alternative for their financial needs. We briefly contemplate the practical application of these new products, offering our insight on their use to facilitate business needs and the indirect impact on national economies.

Placing the industry issues in the context of facilitating the evolution of Islamic finance is the focus of Chapter 5, Industry Issues in Context. Our discussion centres on the markets' desire to achieve some level of Shariah standardization and the impact of how scholars can interpret Shariah principles in the near and distant future. As the markets for Islamic finance mature and new competitors enter the market, the dynamics of competition will change, forcing institutions to differentiate their Shariah-based products in new ways. We pose the question: is there a new criterion for measuring the performance of Shariah-based products/institutions?, hoping to show that Islamic banks and Islamic finance need to be assessed on grounds different from those of traditional banks.

Throughout the book, we will endeavour to show that unlike traditional banks that spend enormous budgets and resources on innovation, Islamic banks face a further challenge. They do not have dedicated departments for product development, market research, process engineering, system development, operational research, back office automation and straight through processing. These activities, requiring as they do enormous financial aid, human resources and time, are harder to justify for Islamic banks, which is why the innovations occurring in the Islamic banking and finance industry demonstrate that creativity and originality do not depend on large investments only, but rather on the will to promote change.

Notes

1   Luis Maronese, Director, Group Corporate Communications, Ithmaar Banking Group, interview with the authors, July, 2008.

2   Top 500 Islamic Finance Institutions, *The Banker*, November 2007, p. 3.

3   Top 500 Islamic Finance Institutions, *The Banker*, November 2008, p. 4.

4   Aziz, Zeti Akhtar, Enhancing the resilience and stability of the Islamic financial system, keynote address to the Institute of International Finance Conference, Kuala Lumpur, November 20, 2008.

5   Laurent, L. (2007) BNP Paribas freezes funds, *Forbes*, August 9, www.forbes.com

1

THE EVOLUTION OF ISLAMIC FINANCE

Islamic finance, more appropriately defined as "Shariah-compliant financial services", is emerging in the first decade of the twenty-first century as an industry in transition. As part of the global financial industry, institutions offering Shariah-compliant financial products are gaining market share over conventional financial institutions due to four factors:

1 Favourable shifts in economic conditions in countries with Muslim populations, creating excess demand from Muslims who do not have adequate access to Shariah-compliant financial services.

2 Cyclical market activities within some Islamic countries that have only been minimally impacted by the economic downturn in the form of transnational commerce between emerging nations.

3 Government support specifically aimed at improving the quality and credibility of the Islamic finance industry.

4 A retreat from US markets by Middle Eastern and global investors who now favour local investments.

Recent Developments in the Industry

In 2008, the Islamic finance industry reached a new high of $639bn, representing 0.7% of the global $900,000bn financial industry.[1] Historically, financial matters based on Shariah principles have been a small part of the global financial community. Over the past four or five decades, the influence of the sociopolitical dynamics of European empires and America's economic dominance pushed Islamic finance into relative obscurity, where it was often practised just under the surface of trade and the financial activities of Muslims living in Islamic and non-Muslim nation states. During the first generation of Islamic finance, the industry was localized, developing within the confines of the communities wanting to conduct financial transactions under Shariah principles. The localized nature of Islamic finance is perhaps the prime contributor to the variations in interpretation of Shariah and the differences in the implementation of banking products in various markets. However, the geopolitical factors shaping the early years of the twenty-first century have created an environment of fertile ground in which the seeds of a new industry have taken root as Islamic finance has become globalized. Strong growth in emerging economies, such as in the Middle East, Southeast Asia and parts of Africa with rapidly growing youth populations, has created a set of conditions conducive to a reaffirmation of Islamic ideals by contemporary Muslims and a rise in demand for finance that conforms to Muslim religious convictions. Figure 1.1 illustrates the developmental stages of Islamic finance as an industry.

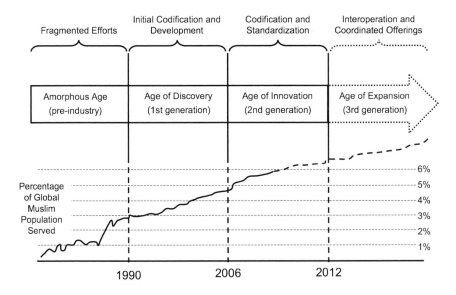

Figure 1.1 Developmental Stages of Islamic Finance as an Industry

Islamic finance is now entering the second generation of developmental stability and product proliferation. The influence of modern Muslim society is having a unique effect on the industry, motivating banks to create new products and be innovative in applying these products to local markets. The increasing demand presents a conundrum for senior management teams, who must choose the type of innovation that will best serve the organization's growth objectives. There are two distinct markets – a rapidly growing demand for Islamic finance in non-served communities and a demand for more sophisticated products in currently served communities. As a result of these two emerging demands, banks are rethinking their product portfolio, brand identity and institutional image.

An example of this trend is the fact that in various conventional markets, such as the UK, the USA, Canada, Australia and Southern Asia, the term "Islamic banking" or "Muslim finance" is being replaced with "Shariah compliant", "Shariah based" or "based on Shariah principles". Sometimes, it is referred to as "ethical banking". Although one can argue that the transposition of the term "Islamic" with "Shariah" is simply an observational shift in the use of words within the popular lexicon, it does, however, reflect a distinct shift in the brand identity of the industry. What is important to note is that the change in brand identity does not equate to an attitudinal change in compliance to Shariah standards, nor does it imply that Islamic ideals are being compromised or reduced. On the contrary, Islamic ideals are becoming the ethical yardstick for the industry and are, to some extent, influencing conventional markets as well. Understanding this shift in brand identity is of paramount importance, as it signals to the market the efforts made by Islamic banks to maintain trustworthiness in the industry for something more than regulated standards. It also signals to customers that Islamic finance is capable of being interpreted differently across diverse social structures, as the change in branding is clearly focused on packaging Islamic finance to be competitive in mixed, non-Muslim-dominated societies. Shariah-compliant banks are altering their image and simultaneously striving not to compromise the moral and ethical foundations of Islamic finance. This rebranding of Islamic finance in Muslim and non-Muslim societies is evident, for example, in the removal of the word "Islamic" or any other such connotative word from the names of banks (for example Gatehouse, Bank of London and The Middle East, Unicorn, UM Financial, University Bank, HSBC Amanah), recrafting the link between religious values and finance, linking finance and banking to a law and ethical set of principles that appear under the umbrella term "Shariah compliant". Table 1.1 illustrates the use (or lack thereof) of the term "Islamic" in the brand identities of new banks.

Table 1.1 New Market Entrants		
New Entrants		
Institution	**Country**	**Started service**
Maybank Islamic	Malaysia	2008
Kuwait International Bank	Kuwait	2007
Dubai Bank	UAE	2007
Bank Islam Brunei Darussalam	Brunei	2006
Bank of London and Middle East	UK	2007
Alliance Islamic Bank	Malaysia	2008
Alliance Bank Malaysia	Malaysia	2007
Al Rajhi Banking & Inv Corp	Malaysia	2007
European Islamic Investment Bank	UK	2006
Cham Bank	Syria	2007
Islamic Bank of Asia	Singapore	2007
Asian Finance Bd	Malaysia	2007
Global Banking Corp	Bahrain	2007
Emirates Global Islamic Bank	Pakistan	2007
FNB Islamic Finance	South Africa	2004
Dawood Islamic Bank Ltd	Pakistan	2007
European Finance House	UK	2008
Ahli United Bank	Bahrain	2007
Omdurman National Bank	Sudan	1993
Gatehouse Bank	UK	2007
RBS Pakistan	Pakistan	2007
Al Hilal Bank	UAE	2008
Fortune Capital House	Bahrain	2008
Yazi Capital BSC	Bahrain	2008
Fajr Investment Advisory	Bahrain	2008
Murabahat Investment Co.	Kuwait	2008
Source: Maris Strategies and *The Banker*		

A contributory factor in the growth of the industry is the emergence of market entrants supported by government shareholders, such as Alinma Bank in Saudi Arabia, Masraf Al Rayan in Qatar and Noor Islamic Bank in the United Arab Emirates. These are not nationalized banks, rather, they are financial institutions with shareholders that happen to be their respective governments. Market growth is coming from many sources, as illustrated in Figure 1.2.

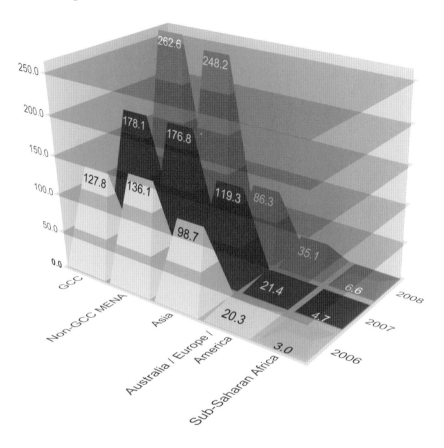

Figure 1.2 Shariah Assets reported by Banks in Billions of US$, by Region

To understand fully the enormous growth of the industry, one must first reflect on a short history of Islamic finance to place the rapidly emerging plethora of Shariah-compliant financial product innovations into the context of an industry transitioning between revolution and evolution. The historical view of Islamic finance is essential to understand the future of the industry, because historical growth curves can be linked to market penetration rates, which can be used by a nation to determine the saturation point of the market's ability to absorb Islamic finance (see Figures 1.3a and 1.3b). As more banks move into a nation, and more Muslims become customers, at some point these markets will reach a maximum number of bankable population.

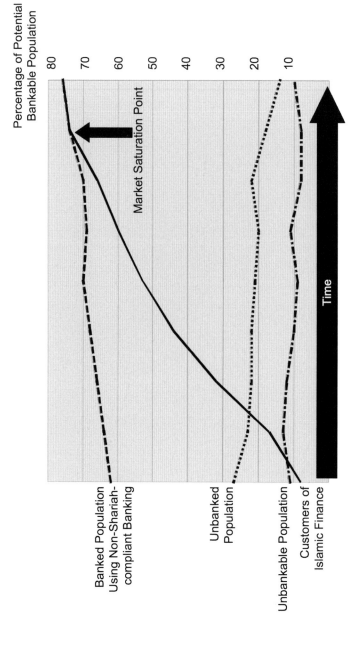

Figures 1.3a Rise of Islamic Finance in Muslim Nations

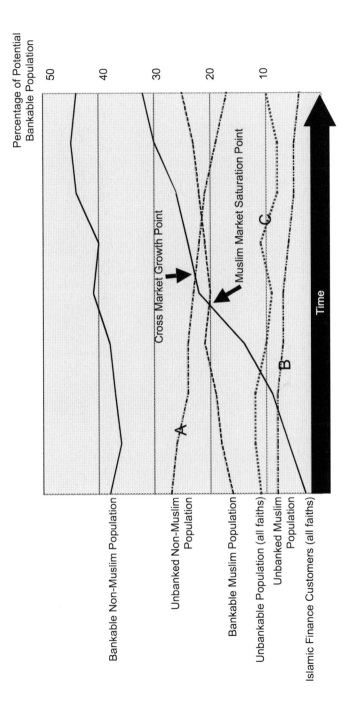

Percentage of Potential
Bankable Population

50

40

30

20

10

Cross Market Growth Point

Muslim Market Saturation Point

A

B

C

Time

Bankable Non-Muslim Population

Unbanked Non-Muslim Population

Bankable Muslim Population

Unbankable Population (all faiths)

Unbanked Muslim Population

Islamic Finance Customers (all faiths)

Figure 1.3b Rise of Islamic Finance in non-Muslim Nations

The subsequent rise of Islamic finance in non-Muslim nations has an underlying dynamic, which is the marked reduction in the unbanked non-Muslim populations (Figure 1.3b, line A). For example, the attraction of non-Muslims to Islamic finance in Africa, parts of the Middle East and regions of the Indian subcontinent can be attributed to the fact that most communities have no access to formal banking systems. Therefore, institutions offering financial services are widely sought after. The rate of decline in unbanked non-Muslim populations is only partially attributable to Islamic finance, the other factor being that as infrastructure to provide Islamic finance is put in place, it also provides access to conventional banking. In Kenya, a predomi-nately non-Muslim country, banks such as Gulf African Bank have indicated that as much as 20% of their customer base is non-Muslim. Similarly, the unbanked Muslim population is also declining (Figure 1.3b, line B), as access to finance is made more convenient. The decline rate, however, is not as great as that which applies to non-Muslims. This is because of the lack of understanding of Shariah-compliant finance by Muslims, who often have to consult with scholars at the local mosque for guidance.

A third trend that can be attributed in part to the proliferation of Shariah-compliant finance is a reduction in the unbankable (all faiths) population of a nation (Figure 1.3b, line C). Unlike the unbanked, who may or may not have stable employment and simply need access to financial services, the unbankable portion of the population have sporadic incomes or long periods of unemployment. Under the financial systems of most nations, people in this category require a banking relationship that operates at little or no cost to the customer. The vast majority of conventional banks ignore this market segment because of the high cost of account opening-closing-openings. Reaching the unbankable population is one of the key challenges for innovation in Islamic finance in the years to come.

The Financial Revolution

The classical definition of the term revolution, as in *"revolvere"*, is to go back to a point previously occupied, or to a point relatively the same. In many cases, the revolution of Islamic finance is based on rediscovering its roots, namely the basic tenets of Shariah principles. Although many Muslims want to practise their faith under the fundamental constructs of Islamic finance, few Muslims have an in-depth understanding of how Islamic finance actually works. This lack of understanding is not confined to Muslims only, as few Christians and non-Christian groups understand the intricacies of modern financial instruments. Indeed, it could be said that the vast majority of people in the world are financially illiterate in their understanding of how financial instruments work to facilitate their lifestyles.

As a result of this lack of customer knowledge of Shariah-based financial instruments, the first generation of Islamic finance products (1990–2006) naturally replicated their conventional counterparts. This was an important step for the industry to gain credibility and establish Islamic finance as a viable alternative to existing forms of financial instruments. Put simply, banks needed to provide a straightforward way for customers to relate to, contrast and compare products with their conventional counterparts. In this way, Islamic financial institutions rediscovered the fundamental tenets of financial transactions based on Shariah principles of equality between parties and reaffirmed the non-exploitative nature inherent in Islamic finance. In the rediscovery of the industry's roots, Islamic financial institutions have laid a solid foundation for the next evolutionary step in the industry.

At the moment, the industry is evolving by moving from the period of rebirth to a new era, where the intention is to set in motion a process for the emergence of new products that are increasingly less like their historical conventional banking counterparts. This next phase in Islamic finance's growth can be labelled the "age of innovation", as numerous institutions are creating new products and/or tailoring existing products to better fit the communities they serve.

The Pillars of Islamic Finance

We define Islamic finance broadly as Shariah compliant, whereby financial transactions are reviewed or previewed by a local Islamic scholar who interprets the word of Shariah law and provides guidance on the degree of compliance that a transaction demonstrates relative to a set of Islamic ideals. The interpretive nature of Shariah law by scholars is the defining quality that demonstrates the adaptability of Islamic finance. The ability to localize interpretations to best suit the needs of the local community is the real strength of Islamic finance and is the basis for innovation. The interoperative nature of Islamic finance makes it adaptable, which in turn drives an innovative approach to establishing equality and fairness in transactions. Let us make it clear that the variability in interpretation of Shariah principles does not in any way compromise the integrity of Islamic finance. As western bankers, analysts and regulators call for higher levels of standardization of Shariah-compliant products, one must realize that the standardization of the structure of products does not mean that the products will be the same. The influence of standardization will be discussed in greater depth in Chapter 5.

Industry watchers, bankers and the media often refer to Islamic finance as simply being "interest free". Although the absence of interest is a defining feature of Islamic finance, we must remember that Shariah-compliant banking is multipurpose, not purely commercial, and strongly equity oriented. Islamic finance strives to accomplish fairness amid parties in a shared risk return model. Ebrahim Fayez Al Shamsi, the CEO of the Emirates Islamic Bank, told the authors that:

> The reason Islamic finance is more stable lies in the fact that while conventional finance is a spectator sport, Islamic finance is a participatory sport. In conventional finance, people leave risk bearing and decision making to a few experts to play in front of them and bear the full responsibility of winning or losing. Islamic finance, meanwhile, spreads risk sharing and decision making among all involved. Conventional finance is like a sphere carried by a mythical Greek god; if he falters, the sphere rolls away and gets lost in space. In Islamic finance, we all carry the sphere and share the burden. More stability would therefore be the result.[3]

Perhaps a more comprehensive definition of Islamic finance is that it is built on principles prescribed by the Holy Qur'an and the Sunnah governing the activities, transactions and interactions initiated by a financial institution between itself and parties requiring various types of financial intermediation. An oversimplification of Islamic finance is to suggest that it is based on the principle "do unto others as you would want them to do unto you". Here, we argue that this latter and simpler definition is not far off.[4]

To understand how innovation will play a fundamental role in the redefinition of the industry, we must first revisit, briefly, the fundamental tenets of Islamic finance.

The Difference between Interest and Profit

Fundamentally, Islamic Shariah principles forbid interest (*riba*) but they do not prohibit all gains on capital. Simply stated, Shariah principles recognize the time value of money (profit) rather than the monetary value of time (interest). Under Shariah philosophy, capital is not costless – capital is a factor of production. Islamic ideals state that capital cannot make a prior or predetermined claim on the productive surplus, which is interpreted as interest.[5] Within the mindset of Islamic thought, the owner of capital can legitimately share the profits made by the entrepreneur. The key distinction is that interest is a predetermined rate of return, while profits contain an element of risk. The profit-sharing ratio may be predetermined based on the contributions of both parties to the overall financing arrangement.

Shariah principles require that the performance of capital must be taken into consideration when rewarding capital. Therefore, in financial terms, the use of capital must add value and not be devoid of risk (Holy Qur'an, 2: 275). Islamic financial transactions are an exchange based on the premise of an equitable transfer of value between two parties, whereby there is equality in sharing risk, an avoidance of exploitation, the exclusion of forbidden products and a clear title to owning and handling of physical goods (assets). In many cases, in modern societies, banks and financial institutions that facilitate the transfer between two parties typically play the role of a hands-off intermediary. Islamic banks act as hands-on intermediaries as they deal and trade in assets purely for the purpose of income generation or profits. Their uniqueness lies in the fact that Islamic banks convert money into assets based on their utility. An Islamic bank must handle the risks associated with the transfer of assets, trades and other ancillary transactions – adhering to the best practices of corporate governance and principles outlined in Shariah law. If the profits generated from these transactions are considered compliant and free of interest, they are said to be permissible or *halal*, and the proceeds are in turn passed on to the depositors as income. If they do not meet Shariah principles, they are considered unsuitable or *haram*, and the Shariah advisers to the institution may, in many cases, assess a penalty to the intermediary to correct the mistake. These principles, when taken in the context of new innovations in Shariah-compliant product development, act to shape not only the product offering but also the way in which the transactions are executed.

It is important to remember that Shariah principles are not only based on the prohibition of interest, they are also designed to avoid unethical practices. Islamic institutions provide customers with the means to facilitate the transfer of value between parties by measuring their intentions against the fundamental social values expressed in the Holy Qur'an and the Sunnah. Therefore, Islamic institutions are set apart from other financial institutions in two ways. They must review their intentions against a moral and ethical lens before they take action, and the products or services they bring to the market must reflect the direct values and beliefs of their customers – ranging from strict fundamentalism to moderate multi-cultural environments. Put simply, Islamic financial institutions consider the needs of the communities they serve in order to create products that reflect the values and beliefs of their customers, unlike non-Muslim institutions that create products with the specific intention of persuading customers to adapt to a new banking behaviour. This distinction is key to understanding the dual strategy of banks as they innovate. Islamic banks incorporate local or community needs in their product design and look for ways to apply the product to other, similar communities or to an economic environment where the product can be employed to service a specific market segment.

From Product to Financial System

For western bankers and non-Muslims, the inevitable question is how can a financial system operate without interest, treat lenders and borrowers equitably and work towards the overall improvement to society? The answer is not simply that Islamic institutions have developed complex profit and loss-sharing mechanisms, nor that, over time, they use interest-like alternatives such as instituting offsetting service charges, or that they act as buying agents from which assets are leased and then transferred at the end of the term. Islamic finance is interpretive, adaptive and, above all, dynamic, in that the interpretation of Shariah law reflects the local culture and social fabric of the communities served, including the varying approaches to interest. One could argue that a Shariah-compliant interpretation is synonymous with innovation in its ability to adapt or incorporate situational variables into product design.

To examine the question of the different underlying promise of Islamic finance as opposed to conventional banking, a few historical considerations are in order. In today's contemporary debate about the viability of Islamic finance on a larger scale, one question often arises: how can an economic system thrive without the charging of interest? To demonstrate how interest is not the underlying factor of economies or banking systems, we need to look at the history of the basic principles that guided Christian economies during the Middle Ages. This raises an interesting point: why have Christian societies jettisoned their adamant stand on fundamental ethical values such as interest? Although it would be interesting to examine the decay of ethics as a foundation for Christian banking in more detail, we will limit ourselves to the relevance of Christian and Muslim traditional values to Islamic financial innovation.

Islamic Finance and Ethical Values

"It was mainly through peaceful trade that the faith of Islam arrived in different countries",[6] noted Gordon Brown, then the UK chancellor of the exchequer. The principles of Islamic finance focus on fair trade, clarity, accuracy and the rights of all parties involved. They recognize and respect the role of the market and the freedom of individuals entering trade.

Shariah-compliant finance follows a strict framework of ethics for the conduct of banking and financial transactions (*halal*), avoiding ambiguities that are defined clearly by a number of prohibitions (*haram*). The most important principle of all transactions is justice, which means a fair and balanced dealing of both parties entering into the transaction. It imposes equal rights and obligations for both parties. Likewise, Shariah-compliant finance encourages and respects truthful and honest merchants conducting trade and transactions in a clear, fair and just way. Cheating, selling defective goods, hiding or misrepresenting the truth, gambling and speculating are forbidden in any type of transaction.

All trades and transactions in Islamic banking and finance have to comply with and conform to Shariah rules, taking into account the effect that the transaction has on both parties. Shariah does not recognize trade or transactions that qualify as *haram*. Any elements that are *haram* render a transaction invalid and unlawful. *Riba* (interest) is the most fundamental cornerstone of Shariah-compliant finance. Interest, including any gain from loan or debt, is forbidden, and the prohibition covers all forms of interest.

There are numerous variations of how Islamic banking is brought to market in which Shariah-compliant products reflect the various schools of Islamic thought. The variations centre on the interpretations of Shariah principles that are universal in nature throughout the Islam. During the Middle Ages, Christian ecclesiastics were fiercely against usury, arguing that it was against the natural order of things – "a sin of cosmic proportions", which was a direct reflection on the Aristotelian view on lending, whereby natural law was of a just equality: whatever was lent was returned, nothing more, nothing less. By the thirteenth century, St Augustine's definition of usury, as practised by anyone who expected to receive back more than the amount lent, was widespread. The Church established cannon law, prohibiting borrowing money where the lender would receive more that the original amount. Critics of various implementations of today's Islamic banking compare the formulaic methods of calculating the time value of money with a method of circumventing cannon law used by European bankers during the Middle Ages known as *contractum trinius*.

It is helpful to understand the history of medieval contracts, which originated using the same set of fundamental beliefs as Muslim finance, in order to appreciate the context of where the value proposition of Islamic banking stands today and the path it may take in the future. Shariah scholars will continue to review the modern adaptations and use of more sophisticated techniques in facilitating interest-free commerce, with an ever watchful eye towards the future. As we can see, the evolution to today's conventional interest-driven banking industry did not happen over one single event, but was a slow gradual process made manifest from within Christian economies to facilitate the monetary needs of a world that was becoming less agrarian and more commerce centric.

The three central issues that altered society's views on usury can be directly linked to the overall value proposition of the process of capital provision:

1 The western world's understanding of time was changing from a cyclical mindset to the recognition of a linear progression. This had direct implications on the value of assets, commodities and money over the time each was used, relative to the use elsewhere.

2 The idea of a just price was also changing, as society's attitude moved from the idea of a fair or ideal price, based on a good's value in its usefulness to the community, to that of prices based on market-driven forces of erratic supply and demand. The Church found that, over time, it was impossible to fight the combined forces of everyday life – as scholars debated, people still needed to eat, farmers to plant and harvest, businesses to engage in commerce and trade.

3 The centralized nature of the Church meant that it concentrated on matters of legal infringements due to its hierarchical structure. This is strikingly different from Islam's decentralization of Shariah principles, whereby local scholars interpret the law that technically reflects the local community. This is the first point of divergence between traditional banking and Islamic banking, one which will lead the two types of banking to become quite different in modern times.

Several other factors that shaped the medieval mindset included the realization that the value of money was affected by supply and demand, whereby over time what was lent might be returned at full face value but was worth less than when it was lent. This line of thinking shifted the debate from simply usury to one of risk, fair use and the generation of profits. In addition, throughout the Renaissance and into the seventeenth century, there was a consistent gradual decline of the influence of the Church in economic affairs.

The Church took little official interest in matters of usury after the seventeenth century. Pope Benedict XIV's encyclical of 1745 stated that the nature of the sin called usury had its proper place and origin in a loan contract, whereby one returns to another only as much as they have received. The act that constitutes a sin rests on the fact that sometimes a creditor desires more than what was given. In 1917, the Code of Canon Law described the act of usury as not in itself illegal to contract for legal interest, unless interest rates were found to be manifestly excessive. Over time, the Christian definition has struggled to make a clear distinction between the cost of capital and interest.

In Islamic finance, the prohibition on interest does not imply that capital is costless – Islam recognizes that capital is an aspect of production. However, it is *haram* to make a prior or predetermined claim on the productive surplus in the form of interest. Under Shariah principles, the owner of capital can legitimately share the profits made by the entrepreneur because it is the ratio of profit sharing not the rate of return itself that is predetermined.

Evolution within the Industry

Like any human endeavour, the Islamic finance industry has its champions and detractors who continually debate the finer points of what is or is not Shariah compliant. Bankers are not Islamic scholars, therefore they cannot be expected to be as well versed on Shariah principles as Shariah scholars. However, regardless of the level at which a banker is engaged in Islamic finance, an individual must be aware of the fundamental building blocks of Islamic economic thought:

- The time value of money is profit, which is acceptable (*halal*), but the monetary value of time is interest (*riba*), which is not acceptable (*haram*). Profit must be generated by acceptable activities, which exclude unacceptable businesses such as gambling, alcoholic beverage products, pornography and others.

- Islamic structures must have an underlying asset backing the deal.

- The sale price of an asset is predetermined in an agreement, and if conditions change and the asset were to become "non-performing", the seller cannot claim more than the fixed sale price. Once fixed, the price of the asset remains fixed.

- A structured financial product is composed of processes and tasks, each of which must be fulfilled in accordance with Shariah principles. If one task does not meet the criteria, the entire process is no longer valid.

So What has Changed? The Need for Financial Engineering

During the first commercial generation of Islamic finance (1990–2006), the tools for Shariah-compliant finance were constructed based on two distinct operating principles: the classical needs of Islamic society in previous centuries as the core principles of product structuring, and a copying of conventional financial products that would be familiar to global customers when comparing Shariah-compliant products with conventional banking products.[7] Now, as we move into the second generation of Islamic finance, Muslim societies and Muslims living in mixed-faith societies are demonstrating a need for greater sophistication in financial products to facilitate the emerging diverse lifestyles of Muslims. Much of the innovation will demand a robust, well-functioning banking infrastructure to guarantee the efficient, safe, reliable and cost-efficient creation and distribution of new products. Many new products introduced in 2007–08 reflect a higher degree of alignment with Muslim societies, governments and business.

A new generation of Islamic finance is being ushered in, one in which the specialization of products will be the market differentiator for Shariah-compliant financial institutions. The change in composition of product design and services packaging is a predictable and logical step for the industry. One of the key factors shaping this need to rethink products is due principally to the cultural differences, political systems and widely varying regulatory structures possible under Shariah interpretations.

The need for financial institutions that can offer a wide variety of services to diverse populations is being fulfilled by two different types of organizations, which share fundamentally similar operating models: wholly Shariah-compliant banks, and conventional banks operating Shariah windows. Typically, the business model adopted by Islamic financial institutions reflects a strong risk-averse ethos. The operating models of these banks reflect the markets in which Islamic finance has been introduced – markets where there are no Shariah-compliant financial institutions. Banks operating under these market conditions have focused on providing basic services to populations eager to embrace Islamic finance. However, in several markets, Muslim populations have been sceptical about the authenticity and trustworthiness of Islamic finance, resulting in banks having to build market awareness in Muslim communities. Banks in the US, the UK and now Europe are learning that when the banking products and providers reach saturation point in the market, customers look for the best value for money in a banking relationship. Customer knowledge of products has reached the point where their level of sophistication demands products that reach beyond basic banking, which means that a bank's business model must change drastically to maintain customers in a competitive environment. For many Islamic banks, the saturation point in their market has not been reached; however, it is not far off, perhaps less than five years. Surprisingly, in Malaysia, it has recently been argued that the religious factor of Shariah compliance as a reason for bank patronage is not conclusive enough to drive Muslims to use Islamic finance.[8] Although this changes the understanding of Muslim behaviour as it has surfaced in Malaysia (and also in Europe), it does not mean that Muslims elsewhere will adopt this attitude. The observation of Muslim customer behaviour highlights the fact that Muslim customers are beginning to evaluate Shariah-compliant banks on new criteria.[9]

An in-depth knowledge of customer behaviour coupled with Shariah principles is therefore the key to market differentiation, which in turn will change the operating model of many Islamic financial institutions as they shift their focus from customer acquisition to customer retention. Knowing when to change the operating model of a retail bank is vital to maintain a competitive edge and capitalize on market opportunities. Creating a business model that is different from that of other Islamic banks and from conventional banks, that is, the ability to offer Shariah-compliant services, is a strategic move to gain market share against a growing number of competitors. The basic change in a bank's business model is to move away from an operating philosophy, where an institution's attitude towards customers is a reactive stance, "we have a Shariah-compliant product so you should do business with us", to a proactive corporate ethos of "what do we have to do to earn your business?" That said, this market shift is concentrated in the maturing Islamic finance markets; whereas the vast majority of Muslims globally have little or no access to financial services.

From an operations perspective, this shift in customer philosophy is easily noted, and banks employing a reactive posture will merely develop a standard suite of products to apply to all customers, while banks opting for a proactive posture will innovate to gain the business. These are two different strategic approaches: the transaction business and the relationship business. Few institutions have the investment capital to do both at a level of quality or competitive price point, as they are often mutually exclusive operating states. A transaction business requires low costs, minimum training in products, and can utilize less skilled employees. Volume is the key, where they take a small fee for processing transactions through their part of a nation's financial infrastructure or interbank network. Competition in many markets for Shariah-compliant services from a reactive transaction bank positions it against larger competitors like HSBC Amanah and Standard Chartered, whose streamlined operations demand that competitors raise the cost of service to a primary concern. Operating targets in this environment will dictate that an Islamic financial institution achieves significant transaction volumes per branch, increases ATM traffic, account origination, card processing and customer service representatives to achieve profitability. Customers attracted by this form of banking are looking for a bank to carry out Shariah-compliant transactions and use services as commodities. Customer loyalty among transaction-seeking customers is relatively low.

The second strategic approach structures the organization and its products to be a relationship business. This model demands a proactive posture when servicing customers whose prime motivations are often convenience and quality of service. The more applicable opportunity for local Islamic financial institutions is to adopt a proactive business model centred on providing financial solutions to customers in the upper half of the economy, and, over time, to develop retail offerings that can be extended to the rising markets and/or the underbanked markets. Relationship banking models require talented employees who can provide financial advice and articulate the principles of Shariah compliance, in addition to executing transactions and tailoring products to fit an individual's needs. This in turn means significant investment in training customer service personnel in skills such as cross-selling, relationship management, customer satisfaction, problem solving, resolution management, risk analysis, phone courtesy, and in-depth product knowledge. That said, a financial solutions-based bank promotes innovation because it must adapt products to meet various lifestyle requirements. It is during the process of tailoring products to meet the needs of customers that a bank can exercise a process to create new products that can be applied across the customer base.

An oversimplification of an Islamic finance institution's market strategy is to grow deposits, increase its portfolio of financing products, build a base of trade financing products, and generate profits or fee income. The first challenge to the Shariah-compliant industry will be to address the issue of a lack of liquidity in the primary and secondary markets. Let us consider the classical definition of liquidity as the ability of an asset to be converted into cash quickly and without any price discount. Put simply, liquidity is the capacity to obtain cash on demand: a bank can increase its liquidity by shortening the average term of its loans. Unfortunately, Islamic banks do not have this option in their strategic toolbox.

Liquidity management in Islamic banks is primarily sourced from consumer deposits. It is a basic fundamental to balance the books by raising enough liability to fund the bank's assets. However, that equilibrium is readily available on a daily basis and Islamic banks need to borrow from the Islamic interbank market. There are always banks with a surplus of liquidity that are ready and willing to lend to banks in need of liquidity. The most popular way is through a *mudarabah* (profit sharing) contract. In this case, the borrower bank would agree to give a share of its profit according to the *mudarabah* ratio. This is similar to the conventional banking way of raising liquidity through selling previously purchased government *sukuk* (bonds bought originally at par at time of issue) in the secondary market to another bank.

Alternatively, an Islamic bank with an asset portfolio in hand (*mudarabah* and *ijarah* (leasing) assets) can sell investment in these assets to other banks acting simply as a broker. Finally, *tawarruq* arrangements (reverse *murabahah* or deferred payment) could be used by Islamic banks to lend or borrow liquidity. Conceptually, the *tawarruq* arrangement purchases an asset based on a negotiated price for subsequent resale of the same asset to a third party to receive cash on a deferred payment basis. The two banks (borrower and lender) select the commodity (gold, silver and so on), purchase the commodity from another bank on a *murabahah* (purchase and resale) basis, and sell it after delivery.

Theoretically, one role of a bank as a facilitator of economic activity is to create liquidity in the markets they serve, as we will discuss in Chapter 2.

The Financial Needs of Muslim Lifestyles are Changing

Consumerism is changing Muslim societies across the world as various economic factors have acted to liberate traditional social hierarchies. For example, young (under 25) college-educated Middle East Muslims are often technologically savvy; they have professional careers, enjoy an active social life and eating out, dress fashionably and consider mobile phones their lifeline. Simultaneously, they also value their faith as Muslims and strive to incorporate basic Islamic tenets into their busy, progressive lives. However, although consumerism is part of their lifestyle, young people have an inherent need to safeguard their Muslim beliefs.

Middle Eastern youths use the internet for shopping; they also use social networking websites to search for Shariah-compliant investment services and distance education services. The consumerist impact of the new generation of Muslims has yielded new products such as the ilkone i800 (variant of the Arabic word for "universe"), the smart new Islamic mobile phone offering features such as establishing Qibla direction (towards the Ka'bah at Mecca) from anywhere in the world, the full text of the Holy Qur'an with English translations (approved by the scholars of Al-Azhar in Egypt), and automatic precise prayer timing anywhere in the world with Azan (call to prayers).[10] Another example of the changing lifestyle choices for Muslims can be seen in services such as Dubai's Tamani Hotel Marina, a hotel that caters to the Muslim values of no alcohol, *halal* food and a donation of a percentage of profits to recognized charities.[11]

Neoclassical consumerism was based on businesses offering products under a regime of profit maximization. Companies produced a vast array of goods ranging from necessities to luxuries and eager consumers purchased items they needed or perhaps simply wanted. During the 1990s, consumerism itself changed, as consumer behaviour is now sovereign, dictating what products are produced. In other words, western societies have shifted from a consumerism based on purchases of "needs" to purchases of "wants". Living beyond one's means has become the norm of societies with access to easy credit. In 2007–08, the world witnessed the folly of this social philosophy.

In order to understand Islamic finance better, we now briefly examine a few differences in the operating models of Islamic institutions and conventional banks, as they equate to adaptation to national and international markets. One adaptation of Islamic banking from its classical roots is the use of the *mudarib udarib* principle, the use of an agent who may appoint another agent to run a business or transaction. In a conventional financial context, this is analogous with subcontracting.

Is Islamic Finance Just Another Variation of Conventional Banking?

To understand how the next generation of Islamic banking products will be different from their conventional banking counterparts, it is necessary to review two key ideas in banking: the rules that banks follow, and how banks make money. It would be naive to think that all conventional banks are the same. Conventional banks follow distinctly different sets of operating principles categorized into two broad classifications: commercial banks and universal banks. Here we are concerned with commercial banks.

Typically, but not in all cases, traditional commercial banking makes money in several ways:

1 as a financial intermediary, whereby a bank receives money from depositors and lends money to individuals and corporations. The interest rate charged on loans is income and the interest rate paid to depositors is cost.

2 by charging for banking services such as foreign exchange, remittances, account management charges, payment transfer fees, business account fees and other services.

3 by selling the financial products of other banks or third parties such as insurance policies or credit services.

4 from punitive charges to customers – designed to curb specific financial behaviours such as bounced cheque fees, or overdrafts that have not been negotiated.

The operating models of commercial banks can trace their origins to Anglo-Saxon ideals that are found characteristically in western countries. The operating philosophy of a commercial bank is governed first by a national regulatory framework to ensure financial fidelity and second by operational guidelines set out by management to ensure a level of financial propriety. Commercial banks of this type operate under a fractional reserve system that enables them to leverage their deposits, they are prohibited in most countries from trading, and their shareholding is severely restricted to a small portion of their net worth. Customers of commercial banks borrow money for various purposes and their ability to repay the extended loans presents a bank with varying degrees of risk. Most customers use the funds loaned to them for their intended purpose, however, some customers do not. Since banks cannot always ensure customer behaviour, because of the cost of doing so, there is a degree of unknown risk that bankers call "moral hazard".

Building the Brand of Islamic Finance

Banks and financial services companies continually seek to reduce their operating costs. The Islamic finance sector is no exception to this operating philosophy as banks adjust their cost structures to respond to economic uncertainties such as the global credit crisis and for growing economies only marginally influenced by external global economic factors. To meet the dichotomy of challenges, financial institutions have reacted by striving to be more efficient and making conservative strategic investments in expanding their operations. As a result of this expansion, most Islamic banks have increased their operating costs by striving for higher quality in documenting their Shariah compliance, and to some extent, those operating in emerging countries have seen higher costs when they take on the added cost of rural distribution. To offset these costs, instead of rewarding customers for their business and loyalty, Islamic banks and financial service providers have presented customers with a vast array of increasing fees and decreasing levels of personalized service. Automation has decreased the personal touch of banking, with a drive to move customers towards the lowest cost operating state.

To encourage customers to adopt more technologically driven banking interactions, numerous banks have adjusted their fee structure slightly to encourage customers to use ATM machines instead of dealing with human tellers. These cost-cutting measures lead to a depersonalized banking experience, in which customers have little emotional connection to the bank's brand. Technologies such as internet banking and SMS banking often add to an erosion of brand as human contact with customers is systematically reduced. New technologies create new channels to market, offering greater flexibility to services, but, in many cases, the true cost is brand value erosion. Shariah-compliant banks are learning that the more commoditized the transaction, the greater the need for clarity in the quality/value equation and an explicit re-establishment of the brand identity. Brand erosion for Islamic institutions has been a minor concern in markets where eager customers await any form of Islamic finance; however, as new competitors move into existing markets, Islamic financial institutions will be required to make significant changes in their market strategies.

While many basic banking transactions can now be handled either at an ATM or online, neither outlet is capable of perceiving, let alone addressing, a customer's fears or frustrations. Therefore, Islamic financial institutions must reinforce key ideals such as Shariah compliance with distribution technologies. Unfortunately, as banks rely more and more on technological outlets for service, there are often fewer helpful and knowledgeable staff in the bank branch to assist customers. In numerous cases, Islamic banks have recognized that educating their customers on Islamic finance is often the key to community acceptance and customer acquisition. Educating customers is compounded when servicing the underbanked and low-tech customers in emerging markets (this covers several market segments), as the added higher cost of distribution requires a dual investment in customer service.

The function of a brand is to make the bank and its services recognizable to potential customers and memorable to existing customers. Conventional banks use three distinct strategies for brand development:

- a broad single brand such as HSBC Amanah

- a mix of group and local brands such as Emirates NBD

- a local brand such as Sharjah Islamic Bank.

Smaller Islamic institutions opt for a local brand or a brand partner in a non-competitive geography if they are trying to expand their market presence. Few Islamic banks have opted to develop a single global brand because it positions them to compete head to head with much larger, better capitalized institutions in these markets. Consequently, most Islamic banks develop a niche brand that appeals to local people and their indigenous needs. For that reason, many institutions offering Shariah-compliant financial products concentrate on specific demographic segments with a clear value proposition. As the competitive landscape of retail banking across the globe continues to evolve, the structure of Shariah-compliant products must adapt to give institutions the capability to enter market segments rapidly and withdraw or change their approach quickly if not successful. Overall, the brand approach of Shariah-compliant institutions has been to develop a single overarching brand identity reflecting a set of common Islamic values; in each market, emphasizing one or more of these values (brand attributes) in specific target market segments.

Research conducted by conventional banks such as Barclays/ABSA in South Africa provides a keen insight for Islamic banks in brand development: "a brand is the balance between the emotional and functional experiences a customer has when they interact with a product or service".[12] In the emerging global economic climate, the brand identity of Shariah-compliant services, and to some extent to the entire market for Islamic finance, must reaffirm Islamic ideals and encapsulate five key attributes:

1 *Confidence:* customers want to know their deposits are safe

2 *Commitment:* customers want to feel that the bank has their best interests at heart

3 *Convenience:* we come to you or you come to us, both great service

4 *Cost:* our fees are designed to fit your lifestyle

5 *Comfort:* our channels will enable you to get our advice when you need it.

Core deposits, financing products, trade financing, payment services and investments are at the heart of a successful Shariah-compliant retail bank. Customers value these services based on three basic criteria: rates, convenience and service quality. Banks lose customers when there is a significant weakness in any of these three areas, yet mere adequacy on the basics will not produce superior results. As the retail banking market for Shariah-compliant services changes over the next five years, an institution's success will increasingly hinge on the quality and breadth of the total relationship with a customer. To succeed, Islamic financial institutions must demonstrate a superior service quality and a higher level of performance to grow a customer relationship from a single point of entry, like the opening of a cheque account, into a durable, profitable, multifaceted relationship.

To meet the new competitive challenges, Shariah-compliant banks must develop their competencies in customer relationship management, lead management, cross-selling and retention. However, many banks have misdirected their efforts, concentrating on retaining and expanding relationships with established customers. A higher return on capital can be achieved by focusing resources on building customer confidence during the first three to six months of new customer relationships.

Competitively, Shariah-compliant banks must focus on defining product packages to match offerings that are better suited to customers' lifestyle needs and encourage multifaceted relationships. Unlike other financial institutions whose deposit product packages are constructed based on internal financial and production considerations, Islamic financial institutions must focus on the needs of prime customer segments with an attention to the details of the banks' requirements of Shariah compliance. Therefore, one key factor that Islamic financial institutions will have to address is the process of Shariah-compliant securitization of new products. Securitization is a process of pooling assets, packaging them into securities, and distributing the securities to investors. To be acceptable to the Shariah construct of having an underlying asset as the underpinning to any securitized product, Islamic institutions focus their concerns on the type, structure and quality of the asset and less on the packaging of the product. Suleiman gives a technical definition of this process: "the process of packaging designated pools of assets with or without credit enhancement into securities, and the sale of these securities to the appropriate investors".[13] In Suleiman's view, assets are pooled to enhance the credit characteristics of the investment (through diversification of credit risk, transaction size, geography and so on) rather than a specific individual asset. The securitization of assets may contain provisions of additional protection for the investors against late payments, prepayments, potential write-offs, as well as cash flow timing mismatches. The primary objective for an Islamic institution beyond simply providing investment diversity to customers is to enable Shariah-compliant financial institutions to increase liquidity by releasing portions of their capital that are otherwise engaged in illiquid projects and trade financing activities.

Globally, there is within banks a predisposition to direct new customers into a standardized blend of deposit-related products, including a current account, credit and/or debit cards, and online banking and bill payment. Although this approach often produces short-term results, it does little in building a long-term relationship, which is imperative for an Islamic bank's competitive strategy. To compete in markets that are reaching the competitive saturation point for Shariah-compliant services, banks must differentiate themselves from larger competitors based on the quality of service, rather than on commoditized pricing. At the core of relationship building is an understanding of cross-selling, that is, knowing when to apply products to specific customer needs. Customer retention is not achieved by increasing the number of products a customer has, rather retention is proportional to the mix of products, ideally with at least one type of product relationship in each of the three domains: deposits, financing products, payment services and investments.

Innovation is the key to successfully building a market for Shariah-compliant financial services by creating product offerings targeted to particular customer segments. The use of an institution's products by customers to fulfil their lifestyles is the key to building brand loyalty. As customers begin to evaluate Shariah-compliant financial services based on the overall value of the relationship, financial institutions must re-evaluate their market strategies and develop a strategic process of continual innovation. It is to this topic that we now turn.

Notes

1   Top 500 Islamic Finance Institutions, *The Banker*, November 2008, p. 4.

2   Anouar, H. (2008) Notable trends in global Islamic finance, *CPI Financial*, September 11, www.cpifinancial.net.

3   Ebrahim Fayez Al Shamsi, CEO Emirates Islamic Bank, interview with the authors, October 2008.

4   See, for reference, Toutounchian, I. (2009) *Islamic Money and Banking: Integrating Money in Capital Theory*, Singapore, John Wiley & Sons.

5   Ariff, M. (1988) Islamic banking, *Asian-Pacific Economic Literature*, **2**(2): 48–64.

6   Speech by the UK's Chancellor of the Exchequer Gordon Brown, at the Islamic Finance and Trade Conference, London, June 13, 2006, www.hm-treasury.gov.uk/speech_chex_130606.htm.

7   Iqbal, M. (2004) Financial engineering and evaluation of new instruments, DLC Lecture, Islamic Development Bank, November, p. 3.

8   Rosly, S.A. and Abu Bakar, Mohd Afandi (2003) Performance of Islamic and mainstream banks in Malaysia, *International Journal of Social Economics*, **30**(12): 1249–65.

9   Haron, Sudin, and Wan Azmi, Wan Nursofiza (2006) Marketing Strategy of Islamic Banks: A Lesson from Malaysia, working paper series 006, *Journal of Islamic Banking and Finance*, January–March.

10 Ilkone Islamic mobile phone, www.ilkoneasia.com/product/i800.php, March 1, 2009.

11 Hotel based on Islamic values and Arab hospitality, Tamani Hotels and Resorts, www.tamani.com/Default.aspx, January 2, 2009.

12 Johansson, U. and Holm, L.S. (2005) Brand management and design management: a nice couple or false friends?, in Schroeder, J.E. and Salzer-Mörling, M. (eds) *Brand Cultures*, London, Routledge, p. 149.

13 Suleiman, A.D. (1998) Islamic Securitisation: Practical Aspects, working paper presented at World Conference on Islamic Banking, July 8–9, p. 1.

2

INNOVATION AND MARKET GROWTH

Markets go up and markets go down. The nature of free-market capitalism is a process of economic expansion and contraction. Movement between economic feast and famine is attributed to a wide range of socioeconomic factors and human frailties, the most easily identifiable being greed. Following a market contraction or collapse, there is often a period of fevered regulation in an attempt to thwart future overzealous speculations. However, over time, the needs of commerce and the ingenuity of bankers slowly erode the criteria for lending and a relaxation of rules ushers in another rise and fall. Let us remember that the motivation of any financial institution is to generate profits for shareholders. Profit generation is also a key motivation of Shariah-compliant banks. However, Islamic banks have an implicit requirement to play a philanthropic-like part in the community – having strong ties to charitable ventures.

Market growth is a result of financial intermediaries supplying a wide range of financial instruments that cater to the commercial needs of business, consumers and governments. Islamic finance has largely been focused in three key areas: retail banking, wholesale banking (providing funds to other financial institutions and commodity transactions) and investment banking products.[1] Within retail banking, there is a fine line between innovation and the simple repackaging of financial products to generate new levels of fee income. The growth in the Islamic finance industry can be attributed to strong growth in the Gulf Cooperation Council (GCC) countries and emerging market economies of Asia, coupled with an emerging youth-based demographic and rapidly growing population. In addition, Muslim investors in these regions are shifting their preferences towards Islamic finance over conventional financial services. What is clear is that as Shariah-compliant financial services become available and Muslim consumers see value for money demonstrated, they combine their need for banking with a self-reaffirmation or awakening of cultural and religious identity.

What is different about Shariah-compliant banks is the underlying principle of equality and fairness in transactions coupled with a sense of a higher purpose to the community. In the past, conventional banks, especially small community banks and building societies, also had a greater interest in the community they served. Evidence of how banks played a role similar to those of today's Islamic banks towards customers and community can be found in documents such as the *Rules for Branch Managers* of Lloyds Banking Company of 1874: "No new current accounts should be opened without knowledge of, or full enquiry into, the circumstances and character of the customer."[2] Like today's Shariah-compliant bank, knowing the customer used to be an important part of understanding how to develop the relationship with the customer and tailor products to meet their lifestyle needs. Western banking has somehow lost this flair.

Another important aspect apparent in the statute of the Lloyds Banking Company of 1874 is an understanding of how to manage a customer relationship: "Attention and courtesy to customers, no less than firmness and discretion, are qualities essential in a good Manager or Banker's Clerk, and this to the poorest depositor as much as to the most important customer."[3] The quality of customer service is often overlooked in contemporary banking as branch volumes increase, while service levels often decline. Shariah-compliant services demand higher levels of customer service, because in many cases, there is a process of educating customers to understand which products best fit their lifestyle choices.

What is clear from previous generations of conventional banking is that, over time, banks change their focus towards more profit generation while slowly reducing customer service levels and discounting their role in the community. Participation in the community is, in many cases, relegated to donations to charities or supporting a specific philanthropic endeavour. During the past 50 years, behavioural guidelines were replaced with the codification and computerization of rules for customer service. One could say that over the past five decades, conventional banks have successfully engineered the humanity out of banking. This is why Shariah-compliant banks seem like a breath of fresh air.

The Next Stage of Market Development

For Islamic finance to achieve the next stage in market maturity, innovation must occur in the following essential areas:

- financial instruments yielding stable income flow

- financial instruments to meet government financing needs

- cover or security for financing, in particular, Shariah-compliant alternatives for penalty on payment defaults

- formulas for pricing Islamic financial products.[4]

It is difficult to assess a meaningful measurement for innovation in Islamic finance that is not distorted by external factors and other market forces. Hence, the easiest mechanism to measure market performance as a baseline in order to factor the value of innovation in Islamic financial institutions is to assess the compound annual growth rate (CAGR). For our purposes, the CAGR is calculated by assessing the growth of revenue and assets of an institution over a four-year period, which represents the available data from most institutions. Theoretically, CAGR describes the rate at which an investment in a bank would have grown if it grew at a steady rate. We are using CAGR as a mechanism to factor variables such as currency fluctuations and market volatility. By measuring the annual growth rates of the revenue and assets of an institution, we can attribute meaningful measurements to market penetration rates as a result of innovation in the introduction of new financial instruments, implementation of new financial infrastructure and new distribution channels (Figure 2.1 and Table 2.1).

Table 2.1 Asset and Revenue Growth Rates of Top 50 Islamic Financial Institutions			
Institutions	Revenue growth %	Asset growth %	Asset size in US$ millions
Bank Melli Iran, Tehran	16.20	11.94	48,470
Kuwait Finance House	42.14	26.30	37,178
Al Rajhi Bank	15.32	16.20	33,348
Bank Saderat Iran, Tehran	−34.29	8.14	32,610
Bank Mellat, Tehran	12.33	13.61	32,534
Bank Tejarat, Tehran	−25.09	8.22	26,340
Bank Sepah, Tehran	24.68	26.29	24,142

Institutions	Revenue growth %	Asset growth %	Asset size in US$ millions
Dubai Islamic Bank, Dubai	42.18	28.60	22,802
Bank Keshavarzi (Agricultural Bank), Tehran	−28.65	11.41	16,298
Parsian Bank	58.11	54.05	15,117
Abu Dhabi Islamic Bank	55.77	36.50	12,063
Al Baraka Banking Group	22.58	18.73	11,167
Saudi British Bank (SAAB)	13.87	17.84	10,521
Bank Rakyat	14.94	13.24	10,397
National Commercial Bank	9.38	15.16	10,358
Riyad Bank	14.50	15.28	9,932
Maybank Islamic	12.40	8.80	7,755
Samba Financial Group	15.84	7.94	6,885
BIMB Holdings	19.36	12.70	6,595
Pasargad Bank	86.77	60.64	6,169
Asya Finans Kurumu	2.20	29.42	5,873
Qatar Islamic Bank	35.81	34.08	5,861
Bank Refah	12.29	17.59	5,787
Bank Al Jazira	24.61	19.09	5,758
Banque Saudi Fransi	13.11	29.78	4,711
Türkiye Finans Katılım Bankası	54.58	54.78	4,703
Investment Dar	43.03	39.93	4,644
Emirates Islamic Bank	96.16	63.97	4,616
Eghtesad Novin Bank	7.57	79.33	4,501
Bank Albilad	68.23	32.75	4,442
Bank Muamalat Malaysia	29.05	14.38	4,094
Public Bank	15.34	19.42	4,079
Ithmaar Bank BSC	77.90	75.03	3,956
QNB Al Islami	23.50	46.14	3,903
Faisal Islamic Bank of Egypt	23.57	10.01	3,805
Arcapita Bank	39.36	43.01	3,792
AMMB Holdings	7.26	6.87	3,672
Gulf Finance House B.S.C.	55.79	51.80	3,508
Kuwait International Bank	−1.55	6.50	3,269
Albarakah Tur	24.76	26.11	3,112
Dubai Bank (Masref Dubai)	14.09	45.65	2,973
AmIslamic Bank	10.93	14.64	2,833

Institutions	Revenue growth %	Asset growth %	Asset size in US$ millions
Islami Bank Bangladesh Limited (IBBL)	20.80	16.99	2,788
International Leasing and Investment Company	18.34	51.90	2,784
Qatar International Islamic Bank, Doha	34.30	19.00	2,734
Sharjah Islamic Bank	55.56	33.11	2,722
Bank Boubyan	61.49	31.44	2,701
CIMB Islamic Bank	90.53	36.91	2,678
Source: Maris Strategies[5]			

However, financial innovation in Shariah-compliant financial services is not a panacea. Many factors shape and reshape the process of innovation across an entire industry, such as politics, economics, cultures, regulations, taxes, environment, ethics, time to market and the internal capabilities of the organization. Perhaps the one factor that has the biggest potential impact on Islamic financial innovation is the changing political and economic order of the world today. Changes in economic and monetary policies, trade agreements and other transnational actions will either limit the cross-border growth of the industry or provide a healthy seedbed for the next generation of products. The cultural variation within Islamic communities is another factor to consider when discussing Islamic financial innovation in a holistic context, as subtle distinctions in the interpretation of Shariah principles by local scholars render some products unacceptable. Conceivably, two factors that have yet to be fully engaged in the Islamic financial innovation discussions are the challenges within regulatory constructs and national taxation.

Shariah-compliant banks, like their conventional counterparts, have a continual need to manage their liquidity needs. Typically, conventional banks rely on interbank money markets that, unfortunately, in most nation states are interest based. The lack of liquidity management options has had a dampening effect on the rate and depth of market growth achievable by innovation within Islamic finance. As a result of the lack of tradable short-term treasury instruments, Shariah-compliant financial institutions cannot channel excess funds and are frequently left holding substantial cash reserves.[6] Therefore, one key innovation that is needed is a financial instrument that acts like an Islamic interbank money market. To attempt to fill the liquidity management gap for Shariah-compliant banks, the Malaysian Interbank Islamic Money Market[7] was established and, in 2002, the Bahrain Monetary Authority established the Liquidity Management Centre.[8]

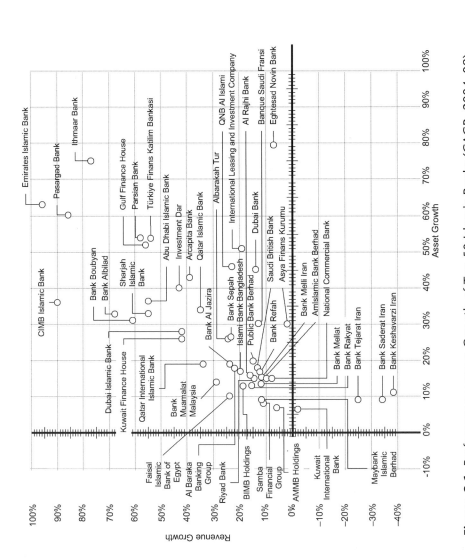

Figure 2.1 Performance versus Growth of Top 50 Islamic Banks (CAGR, 2004–08)

The structure of Islamic finance will be shaped by four key factors: customer demand, technological invention, regulatory structures, and innovation. Innovation is not simply creating new products; rather, innovation needs to occur at many levels in order to propel the industry into its next generation of growth. In the context of Islamic finance, there are numerous forms of innovation: market (*sukuk*), product (Shariah-compliant credit cards and exchange traded funds), service (banking for women entrepreneurs), quality (high touch banking), infrastructure (for example payment systems), back office (transaction processing), and distribution (such as mobile phone banking).

Innovation in Islamic finance is a matter of developing a competitive advantage over other Shariah-compliant organizations and conventional financial services providers. To gain a competitive advantage, Shariah-compliant organizations must establish superior design and delivery of their products or services. Competitive advantage is the result of applying specialized skills, assets and capabilities in a way that provides clearly defined creative solutions to problems, thus the outcome is innovation. Innovation is not the goal; rather, capitalizing on innovation by optimally utilizing internal resources and capabilities to exploit external opportunities at a profit that is acceptable to shareholders, while performing a fair and equitable service to the community is the ultimate ambition for Islamic innovation.

For innovation to flourish, there needs to be increasing levels of market liberalization, such as found in Malaysia, with financial products ranging from unit trusts, equities, structured products, derivatives, exchange-traded funds, fund management, and stockbroking services.[9] Specialized products such as *sukuk* (bonds) have been widely used by financial institutions in Malaysia in many forms, including a sovereign *sukuk* and a global corporate *sukuk*. Although several sources may claim to have invented the *sukuk* product, Malaysia has indeed been prolific in implementing it. Malaysia has also experimented and subsequently introduced innovations such as a healthcare REIT (real estate investment trust) and a plantation REIT.

The success of Malaysia's implementation of Islamic finance is due to three key factors:

- incremental market liberalization

- the integration of key structural components

- determined product experimentation by financial institutions.

The liberalization of Malaysia's markets is part of a process by which increased adjustments (or reforms) were applied to four key economic mechanisms:

- macroeconomic stabilization (such as inflation controls)
- the privatization of government-run industries
- the removal of exchange controls
- trade liberalization.

The goal of market liberalization in emerging Islamic markets is to stabilize inflation while liberalizing trade. Henry reminds us that the product of liberalization is a reduction in the cost of capital,[10] which, in the case of the emerging Islamic economies, is essential in order to create an economic climate for the next generation of Islamic financial innovation. This requires the integration of key structural components such as the Islamic banking sector, the Islamic debt capital and equity market, the Islamic money market and the *takaful* (insurance) industry.[11]

Ahmed Moola, head of Islamic banking at ABSA, South Africa, believes that there is a growing level of product sophistication as institutions move away from the typical conventional product mix towards more "de novo" products:

> The necessity to replicate the economic equivalents of conventional banking products in Islamic finance will soon be outlived. In order for Islamic banking to become more competitive, certain hurdles will have to be overcome and certain barriers crossed with regard to the suite of products offered. Banks are currently using the principles of Shariah as a basis to develop products, while conforming to conventional regulations and legislation. The end product would be expected to have more of the characteristics usually associated with equity rather than debt. Most of such products would generally exist in the areas of investment banking and the top end of the high net worth market. The barometer of the migration towards this next generation will be determined by the extent of the product or products' broad acceptance, that is, Muslims and non-Muslims alike.[12]

The Middle East is the early epicentre in the demand for Shariah-compliant banking services. The evolution of Islamic finance in the Middle East is creating the necessary conditions for a new generation of Shariah-compliant financial products. Ebrahim Fayez Al Shamsi, CEO of the Emirates Islamic Bank, notes the relationship between traditional Islamic products and conventional products as the baseline from which to build the next generation of products and services:

Mimicking conventional finance started with *murabahah*. Now *murabahah* has taken a backstage position and other modes of finance are taking precedence. The era of *murabahah* started to wind down during the late 1990s. It has been followed by the exploration of simple Islamic financial products, which involve the use of a single contract. As the industry became more sophisticated, mixing and matching contracts has become the main source of innovation through the process of product development and structuring.[13]

However, product structuring requires harmonized efforts from a team of Shariah law and finance experts in order to develop and structure new products with proper documentation (contracts, prospectuses, MOUs and so on). Islamic banks are gradually adopting this approach, for example at its inception, the Emirates Islamic Bank formed a product development and structuring team, which is gradually growing in numbers and expertise. The team's first job is to ensure the presence of bank management that are aware of the requirements for future developments in the industry.

In Ebrahim Fayez Al Shamsi's viewpoint, Islamic finance has already moved beyond mimicking its conventional counterpart. Much of the conversion between Islamic and conventional finance is happening in the other direction. Conventional banks are developing and marketing Islamic financial products, joining *sukuk* issues, and forming Shariah-compliant syndicates and other Islamic financial activities in order to benefit from the resulting profits.

Shariah-compliant institutions are therefore developing diversification strategies along two different paths: product diversity and market diversity. Product diversity is addressed by the creation of new products such as consumer financing or small business financing and the entry into previously unused products such as banks offering Islamic insurance, securities dealing or starting an investment group. So there is a great degree of synergy between these views about innovation; now it is necessary to put these into practice.

Product Innovation

The next stage in the growth of Islamic finance will be predicated on the industry's ability to innovate financial instruments. Bank executives often associate innovation with the creation of new technology. However, technology only plays a small part in what is truly innovative. How an Islamic bank applies technology is innovation, whereas invention is the creation of a technology, not innovation. Many Shariah-compliant financial products offered today by Islamic banks are replications of conventional products. These products, if applied in new ways to new market segments, constitute innovation even though nothing new has been invented. Innovation lies in the application of a new product or a technology to a specific market opportunity, such as a lifestyle, or to a explicit socio-economic problem such as the need for small business financing (micro-financing). Although one could argue that the difference between invention and innovation is purely semantics, most senior banks can readily recite numerous failed IT projects that stand as a testament to when banks do not fully understand this fundamental difference.

Islamic financial innovation centres on creating sustainable value with Muslim and non-Muslim customers; this, in turn, becomes a key market differentiator for institutions offering Shariah-compliant services. The distinction between invention and innovation becomes more important as the nature of competition changes for Shariah-compliant products and services. Ebrahim Fayez Al Shamsi, CEO of the Emirates Islamic Bank, stated:

> The top management in such an industry knows that they are working in an increasingly competitive environment. Because Islamic finance is so successful and because the UAE prefers to keep its markets open to newcomers, Islamic finance will continue to face competition from its conventional counterparts as well as from new entrants of Islamic banks and financial companies. Increasing competition can be credited for the significant efficiency gains and the higher resilience that the industry has been able to acquire.[14]

New banks, conventional banks offering Shariah-compliant products and non-banks providing Shariah-compliant services will change the composition of competition as banks will change their focus towards innovation rather than simply implementing new technology. Banking software is rapidly becoming Shariah compliant, which in turn will become commoditized over time at a progressively lower cost. Shariah-compliant software is quickly approaching the price point whereby even the smallest institutions can develop a suite of Shariah-compliant product offerings. As more products are introduced into the market, customers have an increasingly harder time determining greater value for their money in banking services. Therefore, innovation will be a key factor for banks to develop their market differentiation to demonstrate direct value to customers.

New Shariah-compliant products are being introduced across the industry as banks, non-banks and other financial services providers are eager to connect with Muslim customers. In markets such as the Middle East, where there is fierce competition for customers, Islamic institutions are continuing to experiment with packaging Shariah-compliant offerings for specific market segments in an effort to attract and retain a substantial market share. Innovations of this type can be seen in bank offerings such as Abu Dhabi Islamic Bank's *wakalah* (power of attorney) deposit account, where depositors' funds are managed individually and are not pooled with funds from other investors. The *wakalah* concept is seen as a viable form of deposit for retail and wholesale customers, offering an approach whereby the institution agrees to manage funds on an individual basis at an expected rate of return. Al Salam Bank Bahrain offers a similar Shariah-compliant *wakalah* deposit account, where investors have options on the duration of the deposit, such as a week, a month, three, six and nine months and a year or more, and profit and capital are maximized and subsequently released or rolled over on maturity.[15] A *wakalah* deposit account employs the concept of an agency agreement where a bank acts as an agent to attain an agreed expected rate of profit for a fixed number of days. The bank acting as an agent therefore monitors the investment daily to ensure the performance of the investment. If, for any reason, there are doubts that profit rate expectations will not be achieved, the agreement is terminated and the deposit plus any profit accrued is returned to the customer. Strategically, banks such the UK's Islamic Bank of Britain, which launched a similar product in April 2008, see financial instruments such as the *wakalah* deposit accounts as a means of increasing a diversified deposit base.[16] Another innovative approach to provide customers with greater flexibility in their banking is using a *wakalah* account as collateral for consumer loan purposes or to obtain a line of credit or credit cards in banks such as Kuwait's Boubyan Bank.[17] For example, Bosna Bank International in Bosnia Herzegovina has devised specialized *wakalah* accounts for targeted lifestyle options or events, such as rent *wakalah* accounts, opened *wakalah* accounts (short term), child *wakalah* accounts, *haj wakalah* accounts, term *wakalah* accounts and *zakat wakalah* accounts.[18]

Innovation in Service

Innovations that focus on service are harder to find in Islamic banks than in their conventional counterparts, because improvements in service quality are generally harder to justify as value-added projects. Obtaining approval to innovate with new products or technology is much easier because they are tangible assets. Improving the quality of service demands that a bank has two key ingredients in place before improvement can begin: talented people and a process discipline that uses customer feedback. Hence, innovations in service typically focus on a specialized niche within a broader set of services or services are designed to bundle existing products into a dedicated offering, such as Dubai Islamic Bank's *Johara* banking, which is designed specifically to address the needs of women's with specialist banking services.[19] The concept of *Johara* is simple: dedicated banking products coupled with a network of privileges such as shopping discounts and health and educational benefits. In 2006, First Gulf Bank (Abu Dhabi) launched a "ladies only" VISA card designed to address the new financial freedom of women in the United Arab Emirates.[20] Numerous Islamic banks are recognizing the changing role that women are playing in the socioeconomic fabric of their nation. As a result, not only are products being designed to meet the requirements of female customers, branches are now available that are exclusively women only – as seen at Emirates Islamic Bank, Dubai Islamic Bank and Sharjah Islamic Bank.

The practical realities of today are that most Islamic banks have not been able to keep up with the demand generated by new customers. For some Islamic banks, customer service is the Achilles heel of their organization in two ways:

- a lack of capacity in quantitative terms, that is, not enough highly skilled people

- a deficit in service quality, that is, they lack customer service representatives with superior customer handling skills.

In the maturing markets for Shariah-compliant services, the total number of Muslims served is reaching saturation point and the nature of competition is changing from product innovation to service innovation. In real terms, the focus of competition for banks will change from account origination to account penetration or cross-selling, that is, the number of products per customer. This change in market approach, where service will be the benchmark for customers, will divide the market between larger institutions that can make significant investments in personnel and small institutions that will have to innovate new ways to leverage their people with technology. Simple cross-selling techniques will not do for smaller or medium-sized Islamic banks under these competitive conditions. Larger institutions can capitalize on their investments in technologies such as customer relationship management (CRM) to target and lead customers to linked product offerings. Larger institutions also have distinct advantages of lower operating costs and larger marketing budgets. Smaller Islamic institutions will have to turn to technological innovations in order to compete, as customers demand products that are more sophisticated.

Islamic financial services innovation will come from having a clear understanding of the bank's actual value proposition to customers. According to Stephen Ranzini, president of University Bank in Ann Arbor, Michigan, smaller Shariah-compliant institutions are shifting their focus from product development to delivering higher quality services, because in the current financial crisis, customers must be assured that the value proposition of Islamic finance is simple, easy to understand and meets the highest level of fiduciary acumen. In Ranzini's view:

> The strength of the Islamic banking model assists in my view of the future, as the risk sharing inherent in it improves my bank's risk management profile. If we do a good job in avoiding risk, our depositors will benefit and more will come to us.[21]

Put simply, Shariah-compliant institutions must structure their services to facilitate the diverse and changing lifestyles of Muslims in their markets. Muslim societies are undergoing significant changes as people become more mobile through immigration and emigration, thus bringing to each market the need for more diversity in product offerings. Even without the mobility factor, one can see significant changes in societal attitudes towards banking products, such as the adoption of high-tech solutions by younger Muslims to facilitate their banking needs. Muslim small businesses are looking for innovation in financing options to grow their businesses locally and internationally. One thing is clear: customers throughout the Middle East have a rising set of expectations as to the services and products that banks need to provide in order to facilitate their lifestyles and changing business requirements.

To be innovative means to develop a wide range of products that cater to the niche demands of specialized customer groups, such as the lifestyles of younger Muslims, professionals whose jobs demand substantial travel, wealthy customers who look for portfolio diversity and families that pool their resources for specific goals. Another area of specialized products must centre on facilitating life events, such as getting married, buying a home, the *hajj* (the Islamic pilgrimage to Mecca), or to manage the *zakat* (charitable donation) deductions required on their savings. As populations become increasingly mobile, special migrant services are required to facilitate remittances back to the home country or to families living in a different part of the same country.

Quality Innovations

How an institution provides its services, composes its products and designs its offering links it with its customers. Quality of service is more relevant to customer retention than any other measure within a bank. For example, the Kuwait Finance House has implemented service quality improvement programmes that specifically reward excellence in service by employees based on explicit quality of delivery criteria. In fact, customers have a high tolerance for disappointment in rates of returns and unmet profit expectations, but they will change banks quickly if they feel service is below par.

Back Office Innovation

One area that will require extensive innovation to be competitive in the long term is reconfiguring the back office operations of an institution. Documentation processes for a product like *murabahah* (which involves the buying and selling of permitted commodities, with the return to the depositor taking the form of profit on such trades) increase the cost of administration, reduce profitability and ultimately affect its perceived value to customers. Perhaps one way of innovating back office operations is to eliminate them or minimize the processes by collaborating with another institution. The act of collaborating with perhaps traditional competitors is termed "co-opetition" by Brandenburger and Nalebuff.[22] Co-opetition opportunities exist in numerous back office operating functions such as foreign exchange, card processing, loan processing, payments, settlements and any function that is not directly valued by the customer. Conventional banks provide "white-labelled" services to each other, whereby one bank supplies excess core and non-core processing capacity to a rival bank. For example, in the UK, Royal Bank of Scotland provides processing services to other financial institutions. The ICICI Bank in India provides a low-cost, high-tech back office in India and can provide remittance services to other banks with Indian expat customers who want to send money back home. The key is learning from conventional banks that all banking is local – customers only want to know how banking services can fulfil their needs, so anything that cannot be directly seen by customers as adding value to their banking relationship is a prime candidate for co-opetition.

The European Islamic Investment Bank (EIIB) now offers a range of Shariah-compliant investment products to perspective partners: UK, European and GCC global equity funds, property investment funds, structured product funds, hedge funds, venture capital and private equity, pension products and life insurance products through *takaful* companies. In the EIIB model, the funds are managed by in-house experts or an external portfolio manger with specialized fund management skills.

Disruptive Innovation

Innovation in Islamic banking and finance is the intentional adoption of an idea made manifest by its practical application. As Islamic banks begin to focus on innovation, they signal a shift in the industry from institutions simply buying technology and setting up shop to moving towards knowledge-based competition. What is holding back the industry today is the risk of failure when applying a product within a given market. Islamic bankers, like their conventional counterparts, are conservative in their approach and do not introduce innovations until they are comfortable that there is an overwhelming chance of success. This approach worked well during the first generation of growth in the industry. However, in the unfolding competitive environment, time becomes the negating factor. Innovation in Islamic banking is about understanding how to apply products, technology and services to a specific set of customer needs. What banks must be aware of concerning technological innovation is how to "fail fast" and reward failure as well as success.

Innovation will be the key differentiator in the market for any organization offering Shariah-based financial services as we enter the second generation of Islamic banking. Perhaps more importantly, innovation will be what sets Islamic banking apart from conventional banking, as Shariah-compliant services become more focused on providing services that directly engage local customers with a specific value proposition. Shariah-compliant financial product innovation is not limited to retail and commercial banking core offerings. It also involves private equity, venture capital, hedge funds and infrastructure or project finance, all of which are devising new investment and financing products to cater for a wide variety of customer segments and business needs.

One barrier to Shariah-compliant product innovation occurs when an institution wishes to offer a transnational product. There is no global regulatory regime for Shariah-compliant products and few initiatives by governments to address cross-border offerings. Therefore, multinational offerings often require an additional layer of development costs in regulatory compliance and legal requirements. That said, compliance initiatives from organizations such as the Islamic Financial Services Board and

the Accounting and Auditing Organization for Islamic Financial Institutions (AAOIFI) are moving the industry in the right direction, towards
making products more transportable at lower cost. Shariah compliancy is
also not a given, as products transcend regional borders as Shariah
scholars may be required to make a product marketable in a local or
regional market.

Sukuk

Sukuk is generally described by industry professionals (mostly conventional bankers) as a Shariah-compliant bond. However, Shariah scholars
argue that a more accurate interpretation would be that a *sukuk* is a
Shariah-compliant investment certificate. The root of the word *sukuk*
comes from the ancient Arabic term *sakk*, which became the Latin word
"cheque", a term of monetary representation with which all bankers are
familiar. Therefore, a *sukuk* represents a fundamental ownership in the
underlying assets, thereby being entitled to a share of any revenues or
profits associated with the proceeds of the sale of any assets. Whereas a
bond represents a contractual debt obligation and an issuer is obliged to
pay interest and the principal to bondholders on a certain specified date, a
sukuk is not bound to the same rules. A *sukuk* provides an investor with
ownership in an underlying Shariah-compliant asset providing some form
of stable income.

A *sukuk* seems familiar to bankers because it is structured using the
same process of conventional securitization. A special purpose vehicle is
constructed to acquire assets and to issue financial claims (proportional
beneficial ownership) on the assets. It is important to remember that a
sukuk is a tradable financial instrument reflecting the value of a specific
asset or a unique collection of assets.

With so many possible combinations of assets, how many types of
sukuk are there in the market? The AAOIFI has issued standards for 14
different types of *sukuk*, classifying some *sukuk* as tradable and others as
non-tradable – ranging from short-term purchase financing to complex
funding of real estate development and industrial project financing.

In November 2007, Sheikh Muhammad Taqi Usmani, chairman of the
AAOIFI, the Bahrain-based organization of Islamic scholars dedicated to
evolving standards in the Islamic finance industry, declared that up to
85% of the *sukuk* issued up to then may not have been fully Shariah
compliant.[23] Sheikh Usmani's comments had two measurable effects on
the *sukuk* market:

1 the volume of business for *sukuk* fell from US$23bn in 2007 to US$14bn
   during 2008

2 Islamic scholars and practitioners re-evaluated the structures of their
   existing *sukuk*.[24]

The sudden drop in *sukuk* issuance as a result of a global retreat in risk
tolerance is requiring Shariah scholars to review their existing *sukuk* structures. The AAOIFI has issued guidelines on *sukuk* in an attempt to provide
greater clarity on its structures. In the AAOIFI's view, *sukuk* structures that
have a purchase undertaking or a guarantee from the *sukuk* issuer to repurchase at a specific price at a future date may not be compliant with a
fundamental Shariah principle of profit and risk sharing.[25]

However, the debate on the fundamental structures of *sukuk* and the
degree to which they meet the criteria for Shariah compliance will no
doubt continue to be a topic of discussion between Shariah scholars.
That said, one structure that appears to stand up to scrutiny is the *ijarah-*
based *sukuk*.

A Standard & Poor's (S&P) report on the *sukuk* market released in
January 2009 indicated that although the volume for *sukuk* fell as a result
of the overall market for credit contracting, the outlook for 2009–10
remains strong.[26] S&P's report provides an indication of the viability of
sukuk as a mechanism of global finance. Therefore, to place *sukuk* issuance
into a context of how it will contribute to market growth, we will briefly
examine the fundamental constructs of *sukuk*.

A *sukuk* is a financial instrument in Islamic finance that acts as a fundamental building block of an institution's product offerings. The principle
behind the *sukuk* is that the holder has an undivided ownership interest in
a particular asset and is therefore entitled to the return generated by that
asset. Characteristically, the *sukuk* structure entails the acquisition of a property asset by a special purpose company, which in turn is an explicit trustee
of the *sukuk* holders. The trustee receives fees as the issuer of the *sukuk*,
while the *sukuk* holders receive a return on investment based on the rental
income of the asset (Figure 2.2). It is important to remember that the *sukuk*
holders take on the credit risk of the underlying lessee. Although the structure of *sukuk* is similar to conventional asset-based securities, the Shariah
principles governing their underlying structure stipulate that income must
be derived from a real business risk, not simply a guaranteed return from a
loan (interest). Therefore, *sukuk* offers businesses a mechanism for finance
that engages investors as part-owners of the underlying asset, so *sukuk* does
not imply a guaranteed return on capital or investment protection.

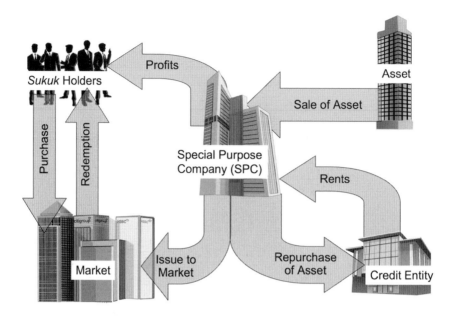

Figure 2.2 Typical *Sukuk* Structure

There are two challenges for *sukuk* offerings under current market conditions:

1 the ability of the underlying assets to generate a Shariah-compliant income stream

2 a lack of liquidity due to a non-existent secondary market.

Once again, under Shariah principles, income generated from sources that produce interest is not acceptable. The most popular income stream is from real estate, whereby rental income generates the desired cash flow-based return to *sukuk* holders, with repurchase obligations to make certain principal repayments on scheduled maturity dates. Practically any asset that can be leased and repurchased can be offered under the *sukuk* structure, such as aircraft, ships, car fleets, infrastructure projects and large capital equipment. Unlike conventional bonds, a *sukuk* gives investors a share in an underlying physical asset, such as leased land, as well as the income that it generates. *Takaful*, where resources must be pooled, benefits because a *sukuk* offers a tradable fixed income component that was previously lacking.

Sukuk structures offer Islamic financial institutions a high degree of flex-ibility due to the broad applicability of *sukuk* as a mechanism for financing business needs and offering diversity to investors. As an investment product, *sukuk* strives to practise the Shariah principle of ensuring that contractual certainty and a mutually beneficial balance between borrowers and lenders is maintained.[27] *Sukuk* offers investors the ability to transfer assets into liquidity without a long legal process and offers a source of cash flow for the originator. *Sukuk* has a maturity that is determined in advance and is backed by an asset (similar to an asset-backed security in conventional finance), which facilitates a return on investment without the payment of interest. The similarity to conventional instruments required a measurement with which conventional bankers and their Islamic counterparts could determine accurately (in relative terms) the performance of the *sukuk*, hence the adoption of LIBOR (London inter-bank offered rate) as a benchmark. However, the widespread use of LIBOR as the reference point for the margin on *sukuk* blurs the distinction between such issues and the world of conventional bonds.

LIBOR is the rate that contributor banks in London offer each other for interbank deposits, that is, an interest rate at which one London bank can borrow money from other banks. LIBOR rates are reported in numerous currencies and are based on complex calculations that incorporate variables such as time, maturity and currency rates. With all this interest-based calculation happening, industry pundits are beginning to question if LIBOR is an appropriate index with which to measure *sukuk*.

The return on a *sukuk* is derived from the yield generated by the lease of an underlying asset, and the authenticity of *sukuk* structures in terms of Shariah compliance rests on the fact that they do not take advantage of interest rate movements. However, under Islamic jurisprudence, investors can receive periodic payments under the *sukuk* structure. This has evolved to a link to LIBOR as the benchmark. Hence, *sukuk* certificates are frequently priced using the same pricing methods as conventional eurobonds.

The credit risk and expected loss relative to the promise made to inves-tors is the basic focus of rating agencies for *sukuk* and similar financial instruments. The report *Understanding Moody's Approach to Unsecured Corporate Sukuk*, published in August 2007, noted that Shariah-compliance adds an extra dimension of considerations in the legal analysis of any material impact on the credit risk profile. Unlike their conventional coun-terparts, *sukuk* assets introduce an additional layer of complexity to rating methodologies. However, rating agencies are reluctant to apply a different rating criterion (although other factors such as the legal regime in which the *sukuk* assets are located must also be considered) to an instrument just because it is Shariah compliant.

Organizations, such as the Bahrain-based Islamic International Rating Agency, have emerged to provide a new dimension of clarity to the level of Shariah compliance of a *sukuk* using a familiarly constructed codific-ation of Shariah Quality Compliance with AAA (SQR) being the highest possible rating and B (SQR) being the lowest possible rating.

Islamic Sukuk and Diversification

Sukuk is important to developing deeper and more liquid Islamic capital markets, which is one fundamental element in Islamic financial innov-ation, as argued by Luis Maronese, the director of group corporate communications at Ithmaar Banking Group:

> The last frontier for financial innovation is in Islamic banking and finance now that most, if not all, of the items on a conventional balance sheet can be readily traded in an established secondary market, notwithstanding any interruptions to such trading that may have occurred in the wake of the subprime crisis. At present, Islamic banking and finance does not have such an established secondary market for many of its finance and capital markets products. Islamic capital market development is the next big opportunity in Islamic finance, even though this will fall prey to, in my opinion, the unfair criticism that Islamic banking and finance will thereby be continuing with its focus on providing comparable products and services to those available in conventional banking and finance. The extent to which there is room for further fundamental innov-ation will emanate from investment banks considering carefully the changing needs of both the sources and users of finance.[28]

Sukuk financial products offer the market marketability (liquidity), ratea-bility (understood by rating agencies), diversity (alternative investment type) and versatility (wide range of application). The question remains: does the industry need a better benchmark for *sukuk*? Industry analysts, academics and bankers will continue to argue both for and against a new, more descriptive benchmark. However, what is clear is that investors need a mechanism that enables them to measure the performance of *sukuk* relative to what they think they are being sold. Thus, as a measurement, LIBOR should be used strictly as a means to approximate the credit risk in pricing. The flexibility, diversity and innovative nature of *sukuk* are demonstrated in the following examples of the broad range of applications in finance.

Perhaps one of the most quoted *sukuk* is that of Germany's federal state of Saxony-Anhalt, which, in 2004, issued a €100m *al ijara sukuk*, which securitized a number of buildings owned by the Ministry of Finance into a 100-year master lease, whereby the assets are rented back to the Ministry of Finance over a five-year period. The *al ijara sukuk* certificate holders receive a variable rent benchmarked to the EURIBOR over the rented period.

The Central Bank of Bahrain regularly issues *sukuk al ijara* and *sukuk al salam* to finance various infrastructure projects in Bahrain. Likewise, Malaysia's global *sukuk*, launched in June 2002, was also backed by an *ijara* lease on a single piece of government property. Along the same lines, the government of Qatar raised money through the $700m Qatar global *sukuk* to finance in part the construction of the Hamad Medical City.

In Dubai, the first airline *sukuk* issued (the Emirates Airlines *sukuk*) closed in July 2005. At $550m, it was the single largest corporate *sukuk* issuance at that time. The *sukuk* was structured with a seven-year tenure as a *musharakah* (joint venture). The proceeds of the issue, listed on the Luxembourg Stock Exchange, will be used to finance the new Emirates Engineering Centre and its headquarters building in Dubai.

Ship financing and civil aviation financing are also popular in the United Arab Emirates (UAE). In 2005, ABC International Bank with Abu Dhabi Commercial Bank created, structured and jointly underwrote a pioneering Islamic ship finance transaction through the issuance of a $26m Al-Safeena *ijara sukuk*. At that time, it was the first issue combining Islamic equity with conventional debt for the same asset. In this case, it was the *Venus Glory*, owned by Pacific Star International Holding Corporation, which is owned by Saudi Aramco, the world's largest oil exporting company.

Along the same lines, the Dubai Civil Aviation Authority joined the *sukuk* issuing groups in 2004, originating a $1bn *sukuk*, the world's largest single *sukuk* issuance in terms of size at that time by any issuer. The proceeds were used to finance the building of a new international terminal and the expansion of existing engineering and other infrastructure. The *musharakah* agreement was in place to develop a new engineering centre and headquarters building on land situated near Dubai's airport. Profit, in the form of lease returns to the UAE, generated from the *musharakah* will be used to pay the periodic distribution on the trust certificates.

In Bahrain, the *istisna'a ijara sukuk* was structured by the Liquidity Management Centre as a Shariah-compliant product. The *sukuk* has a five-year term, offering a quarterly profit distribution with the proceeds used to finance the development and construction of the Financial Centre. This corresponds to the first phase of the Bahrain Financial Harbour project comprising the Dual Towers, the Financial Mall and the Harbour House. The 2006 Dubai World *sukuk*, developed by the Nakheel Group to finance the three palm-shaped islands off Dubai's coast, sold the world's largest Islamic bond after increasing its size by more than 40% to $3.52 billion. The *sukuk* has been listed on the Dubai International Financial Exchange.

In 2007, global marine terminal operator DP World priced a $1.75bn conventional bond and a $1.5bn *sukuk*. DP World is the first issuer to list both conventional and Islamic debt securities on the Dubai International Financial Exchange. This $1.5bn, 10-year *sukuk* is attracting demand globally. For the first time, US investors had the opportunity to subscribe to a UAE corporate-rated *sukuk*. The innovation of DP World's *sukuk* is that it is partly convertible to shares in the event the group lists through an initial public offering, thus becoming the first convertible instrument in the Islamic finance market.

In March 2008, Saudi Hollandi Bank and Taajeer Company announced the successful closing of Taajeer's debut Islamic *sukuk* issue. The closing marked the first time that a private company had issued an Islamic *sukuk* in the Saudi market. Saudi Hollandi Bank served as sole lead manager and book runner for the floating rate note with a 5-year tenure *sukuk*, which attracted 50% more subscriptions than Taajeer had decided to raise.

The first and only *sukuk* to have originated from the USA tapped the market in 2006. The unique feature of the East Cameron Gas *sukuk* was that it was both the first Shariah-compliant gas-backed securitization and the first Islamic securitization rated by S&P. The $165.7m *musharakah*-structured *sukuk* originated from Houston-based East Cameron Partners, whose reserves are located in the shallow waters off the shores of Louisiana.

The year 2008 was the first challenge for *sukuk*, as the world credit crisis and reinterpretations of *sukuk* structures by scholars brought issuance to a fraction of the volume enjoyed earlier in the year. Beyond these two factors, the process of structuring Shariah-compliant products remains slow and labour intensive. The process of structuring *sukuk* products is one of the main challenges in Islamic finance.

Honing the Innovation Process

Conventional securitization is virtually absent in Islamic countries that operate under Shariah principles. The rising interest in Shariah-compliant investments provides a unique opportunity for Muslim nations because it provides a means to advance the development of their capital markets. Innovation in structuring Shariah-compliant products is essential to expand Islamic capital markets. By innovating new financial instruments and other alternative modes of financial intermediation, Islamic nations will also attract foreign direct investment. Hesse et al. note how new innovations in Shariah-compliant finance add to the range of global financial offerings to investors:

> Islamic securitisation also complements the conventional ABS [asset-backed securitization] universe as an alternative and more diversified funding option that broadens the pricing spectrum and asset supply, as high demand for alternative investment products causes greater lending width.[29]

The key idea is that all Islamic financial innovation must be secured with an underlying asset as the core of the transaction. Unfortunately, for innovations such as *sukuk*, the markets for Shariah-compliant products are beset by illiquidity in the secondary market. With the current level of *sukuk* issuance falling as a result of the global slowdown, the volume of issues by corporates and public sector entities remains fractional when contrasted with the global fixed income markets. To date, there are only a small number of *sukuk* issuers specializing in a narrow set of asset-type transactions, which limits the appeal of these products to only the most diverse of investors. The lack of *sukuk* diversity, coupled with the fact that Islamic capital markets are largely local with few regional offerings, limits the appeal to global investors. What is needed is technological innovation to link these markets together in a manner that makes *sukuk* more accessible to investors across all local markets.

Thus, the need for innovation in the *sukuk* product range centres on two key issues: a lack of liquidity and localization of issuance. To innovate requires the creation of a wider range of deal types with shorter maturity tenures (currently 3, 5 and 10 years) to make them applicable to money market-like instruments and to link these markets together technologically to increase overall access to lower cost deals. However, with the interconnection of these markets comes the need to provide higher quality supervision across geopolitical borders. Supervisory harmonization across national boundaries is never easy, and this, coupled with Shariah-compliant governance issues, will demand a consensus on a set of broadly defined guidelines on how Shariah-compliant products will satisfy multinational regulatory requirements.

Islamic Sovereign Securities

Adding product depth to the Islamic finance marketplace is the issuance of *sukuk* based on sovereign debt obligations. Malaysia, Bahrain and Qatar have been market leaders in restructuring public debt in a Shariah-compliant way. The Malaysian government has been issuing traditionally labelled Islamic bonds since the 1980s. Sovereign securities that are Shariah compliant enable the nation states of the Organization of Islamic Conference, which are asset rich and often cash poor, to monetize their existing assets.[30] Typically, banks that acquire sovereign *sukuk* hold them until maturity, rarely trading them, which in many cases restricts liquidity and to some extent makes raising money from the public more difficult.[31] According to Alvi, sovereign *sukuk* provide an essential tool to manage domestic money supply and credit extension of Islamic banks.[32] An analysis of the global market for *sukuk* reveals that sovereign *sukuk* comprises approximately one-third of the marketplace. The lion's share of sovereign *sukuk* issue uses a floating rate catering to the needs of liquidity-rich Islamic banks looking for assets, with a lack of issues along with a shallow investor base. However, to increase diversity within the market and to offer more options for liquidity, short tenure issues are needed. Table 2.2 illustrates the issues over the past decade.

Table 2.2 *Sukuk* Issues, Value and Tenure				
Government	Amount (million)	Tenure	Sukuk type	Year
Bahrain Monetary Agency (BMA) #1	US$100	5 years	Ijarah	2001
Malaysia	US$600	5-year bullet	Ijarah (FRN)	2002
Bahrain Monetary Agency #2	US$70	3 years	Ijarah	2002
State of Qatar	US$700	7-year amortizing	Ijarah (FRN)	2003
Bahrain Monetary Agency #3	US$80	5 years	Ijarah	2002
Bahrain Monetary Agency #4	US$50	3 years	Ijarah	2002
Bahrain Monetary Agency #5	US$80	3 years	Ijarah	2003
Bahrain Monetary Agency #6	US$100	5 years	Ijarah	2003
Bahrain Monetary Agency #7	US$250	5-year bullet	Ijarah (FRN)	2003
Bahrain Monetary Agency #8	US$50	3 years	Ijarah	2003
State of Saxony, Germany	US$100	5-year bullet	Ijarah (fixed)	2004
Bahrain Monetary Agency #9	US$250	5 years	Ijarah	2004
Bahrain Monetary Agency #10	US$106	10 years	Ijarah	2004

Government	Amount (million)	Tenure	Sukuk type	Year
Government of Dubai	US$1,000	5-year bullet	Ijarah (FRN)	2004
Government of Pakistan	US$500	5-year bullet	Ijarah (FRN)	2005
BMA Short Term Sukuk 1	US$27	6 months	Ijarah	2005
BMA Short Term Sukuk 2	US$27	6 months	Ijarah	2005
BMA Short Term Sukuk 3	US$27	6 months	Ijarah	2005
BMA Short Term Sukuk 4	US$27	6 months	Ijarah	2005
Brunei	US$70	91 days	Ijarah	2006
Brunei	US$80	91 days	Ijarah	2007
Brunei	US$35	91 days	Ijarah	2008
Central Bank of Bahrain (formerly BMA)	BHD 6	91 days	Al-Salam	2008
Brunei	US$165	91 days	Ijarah	2009

Source: Standard Chartered Bank, Global Investment House, Zawya Dow Jones and the *Brunei Times*

Bahrain and Brunei are issuing fixed-rate short tenure (Brunei, 91 days) *sukuk* at regular intervals,[33] which could be used for bank liquidity management. Continuous government issues with regular and planned auctions are fundamental to the next level of Islamic finance market development.

Islamic Bank Cards

The term Islamic credit cards, increasingly used interchangeably to describe all types of bank cards, is a misnomer for a simple, convenient card-based financial product that is designed to facilitate payments in the modern world. Islamic bank cards include prepaid cards, debit cards, credit cards, credit-like cards and loyalty cards. For our purposes here, we will review bank cards as a broad subject, with specific attention to the formation of Islamic credit cards to understand why they are and will continue to be an important asset in a bank's portfolio of products. Consumer behaviour models typically link income, consumer confidence and social class as key indicators to purchasing behaviour. Empirical studies and databases of Muslim consumer behaviour are almost non-existent or rarely found by Shariah-compliant financial institutions when developing products. Consumer behaviour within a social class or, more precisely, socioeconomic market segment, is to some extent predictable as a means of understanding the acquisition of financial products and their subsequent use.

Bank cards are simple payment devices that enable consumers to make convenient purchases. The use of bank cards is directly proportional to consumers' trust in the payment mediator (MasterCard, VISA, American Express and so on) and the means by which the payment is handled or processed. Confidence in the processing of card payments is often irrational or derived from a perceived fidelity in the transactions. For example, consumers are less trusting of cards processed by merchants using the paper-based embossing system versus an electronic modem-based point of sale device. Both are legitimate forms of processes, but the paper-based system is often equated with credit card fraud, and so is perceived by customers to be less reliable.

Responsible use of credit as a tool
However, bank cards are also a source of controversy among Islamic scholars regarding the degree to which cards are equated with the charging of interest. Conventional credit cards are based on agreements that include clauses on interest, whereby some cards charge interest on the balance at the time of purchase and others only charge interest on any unpaid balance after the payment due date. Liberal interpretation by Shariah scholars justifies using conventional credit cards by acknowledging the convenience of credit cards in facilitating payment in day-to-day life as long as the user intends to pay the balance at the end of the month to avoid any interest charges (*riba*). However, liberal western Muslims have also interpreted this to understand that if payments are late and interest charges are incurred, an identical payment of the interest to *zakat* will atone for their transgression.

Shariah-compliant financial institutions in Southeast Asia have structured credit cards on the *bai al inah* (sell and buy back) contract model, which is also controversial in the eyes of Middle Eastern interpretations of Shariah principles in that this structure appears to mask the charging of interest in a different form. A vast majority of Shariah scholars in the Middle East have rejected the *bai al inah* contract model. Hence, Middle Eastern banks have opted for a different approach to structure credit cards by charging for a guarantee on payments and recovering such costs as administrative and operational expenses.

One example of a credit card is the Emirate Islamic Bank's credit card, which contains an annual service charge imposed depending on the type of card. It requires the minimum payment of 10% of outstanding monthly totals, and there is a credit limit. Similarly, the Bank Islamic Malaysia card is based on three contracts – *bai al inah* (buy back), *wadiah* (deposit), and *qard al hassan* (benevolent loan). The bank sells its customer a piece of land at a set cash price and buys it back at a lower price.

Prepaid cards

Prepaid cards are a natural innovation for Muslims because they neatly remove the issue of interest while providing a convenient modern way to facilitate payments in secular societies. Prepaid cards are a simple substitute for cash, not a negotiated loan, so there are no interest charges associated with carrying an outstanding balance. Monies are preloaded onto the card and purchases reduce the balance until funds are exhausted. The key to implementing this type of payment scheme is to target a specific market segment. During 2007, Bank Islam's Tourist Friend MasterCard Unembossed Prepaid Card was launched in conjunction with the national campaign MasterCard Visit Malaysia Year Privileges Program that enabled card holders to take advantage of discounts at 400 Tourist Friend merchants and 20 retail chains.[34]

Likewise, in July 2008, Sharjah Islamic Bank launched a prepaid Jeans Card, the first Islamic VISA prepaid card.[35] In August 2008, Cordoba Financial Group launched the UK's first Shariah-compliant prepaid card (Cordoba Gold MasterCard), providing Muslims with an easy to use, interest-free payment mechanism.[36] Funds must be preloaded onto the card before they can be spent, eliminating borrowing or lending, so interest (*riba*) is not a factor. The preloading of funds also eliminates overdraft charges, interest on overdrafts and late payment fees. In addition, a card preloaded with funds does not require a credit check or an associated bank account.

Developing features and functions that are specific to a collection of Islamic ideals such as charity or convenience of use is an effective innovation on how to apply prepaid cards to changing Muslim lifestyles. As Islamic financial institutions act to engage more customers further down the economic pyramid, knowing what features appeal to target market segments is the key to supplemental payment offerings. One example of a targeted approach to prepaid cards is the Hajj & Umra Card issued by Kuwait Finance House, which donates 0.5% of every purchase made to send needy people to *hajj* and *umrah*.[37] This card, targeted at middle-class people, enables customers to contribute to the greater good within society with a degree of anonymity. In Saudi Arabia, National Commercial Bank has additional features linked to its Shariah-compliant prepaid card, such as easy subscription to satellite TV, travel insurance and purchase insurance.

Debit cards

To respond to the needs of Muslim customers, VISA and MasterCard have both launched initiatives to provide Shariah-compliant debit card payment systems. Shariah-compliant financial institutions, such as Lebanese Islamic Bank,[38] have learned from the UK's Co-operative Bank's affinity cards. Lebanese Islamic Bank launched a similar affinity debit card as a vehicle for *zakat* – a tax on wealth rather than spending, in which the bank acts as an independent agent and can contribute to a charity on behalf of individual card holders, thus offsetting against personal *zakat* contributions.[39] An individual's contribution toward *zakat* can be reflected on their annual statement in the same way that individuals collect airline miles or loyalty points. In June 2008, MasterCard and EONCAP Islamic Bank launched the Islamic debit MasterCard, providing access to ATMs and Malaysia's PayPass systems.[40] Lebanese Islamic Bank offers a Bankernet debit card, in Lebanese pounds or US dollars, which can be used to consolidate payments on monthly bills as well as withdrawing cash from any ATM.[41]

Credit cards

Perhaps one of most ingenious (and most controversial) developments in Islamic finance is the Shariah-compliant credit card. An elegant piece of financial engineering, an Islamic credit card provides Muslims with flexibility to practise their beliefs while participating in the global economy. Typically, Muslims have relied on cash or bank cards that simply debit their accounts. Shariah-compliant credit cards fall into three broad structural categories:

1   the bank provides a line of credit to the card holder, subsequently charging a monthly or yearly usage fee tied to the outstanding balance of the line of credit

2   a customer is allowed to buy an item with a card, the bank purchases the item and then resells it to the card holder at a higher price

3   a lease-purchase agreement where the bank holds the title to the purchased item until the card holder makes the final payment.

Industry analysts and media reporters often equate the structures for repayment as a simple exercise in creating an interest-like revolving credit card.

Several structures are used to underpin the process of using a Shariah-compliant credit card. In most cases, card holders can expect to pay a fee (usually 5–10% of the outstanding balance), which is similarly structured to that of a conventional revolving credit card. Another factor, which is unlike conventional credit cards, is that card holders will characteristically be required to secure the line of credit with a deposit account in the bank. Theoretically, the deposit is to offset profits against the fees charged to access and use the line of credit. The concept is similar to mortgage offsetting accounts available in conventional markets, whereby interest owed to the customer for their deposits is subtracted from interest owed to the bank from a customer's unpaid balance of their mortgage loan. The customer pays the net difference between their savings rate and the loan rate. For example, if a customer has a mortgage of US$110,000 at 6.5% interest and deposits of $50,000 at 4.0% interest, the actual loan amount offset is $60,000 at 6.5% interest, due as an instalment at the end of the monthly billing period. In a similar fashion, Shariah-compliant cards use the deposit to offset usage fees by simply generating profits from the customer's deposits, which in turn are shared between the financial institution and the customer at an agreed ratio.

When contrasting Shariah-compliant credit cards with their conventional counterparts, several key factors must be considered:

- interest is not charged

- collateral is required via an underlying deposit or an undated cheque

- a fixed profit margin is shared between the institution and the customer

- late payment fees apply to outstanding balances.

The underlying contract structure is the primary difference between Shariah-compliant credit cards, which are leased based, and conventional cards, which are loan based. Under a Shariah-compliant structure, when the customer initiates a credit card purchase, the bank buys the item and leases it back to the customer. One other caveat of the Shariah-compliant card is the prohibition of purchases such as alcohol, tobacco, gambling, pork and sexually related items.

Responding to the need for clarity in Shariah-compliant credit card structures, the AAOIFI issued a standard to be used as a guideline during the construction of card products. To summarize AAOIFI's standards, a credit card is a revolving line of credit, with a credit limit used within a credit period determined by the issuer of the card. Card holders can elect to pay for purchases of goods and services, or withdraw cash within the designated credit limit. It is also a means of payment. Typically, when a card holder makes a purchase, there is a grace period in which repayment is made without penalty with no interest due. If the card holder elects to defer payment into a subsequent period, there is an interest charge assessed on the unpaid balance. A Shariah-complaint card is different from a conventional credit card, in that when customers elect to defer payment, the card issuer requires a deposit account, which is removed from the customer and invested under a *mudarabah* (profit sharing) structure. Any profit accruing on this amount will be shared between the card holder and the institution according to specific predetermined percentages. In all instances, like other Shariah-compliant products, the underlying structure and financial product strives to have an asset at the heart of the financial transaction.

The other half of the credit card equation is the set of rules attributed to the issuing institution. These can be summarized as follows:

- institutions can hold membership in international credit card regulatory organizations, provided the institutions avoid any infringements of Shariah law

- institutions can pay membership fees, service charges and other fees to international credit card regulatory organizations, provided that these transactions are free of direct and indirect interest payments

- issuing institutions are permitted to charge a commission to the party accepting the credit card, at a percentage of the purchase price of the items and services purchased using the card

- card holders can be charged a membership fee, renewal fee and replacement fee.

The three most popular structures of Shariah-compliant cards are:

- *Kafalah:* the card issuer is the guarantor (*kafil*) for the card holder on behalf of the merchant for all the liability (*dayn*) that occurred as a result of the transactions between the card holder and the merchant, and or cash withdrawal from other banks or ATMs (not from the bank or ATM of the card issuer). On this guarantee agreement, the card issuer will receive a fee (*kafalah bi ujrah*).

- *Qardh:* card holders act as the lender (*muqridh*) to the card holder (*muqtaridh*) through the cash withdrawal from the bank or ATM of the card issuer.

- *Ijarah:* the card issuer is the service provider of the payment system and services to the card holder; for this service, the card holder is required to pay a certain amount of membership fee.

The Qatar Islamic Bank (QIB) launched a Shariah-compliant credit card (Alysr) providing card holders with an automatic credit limit of QR20,000 and repayment options of 10% on the balance each month. Card holders pay a monthly fee of QR125 and 3% commission on cash withdrawals. Each transaction generates a QR1 payment by the bank (not charged to the card holder) to the *zakat* committee as a charitable contribution. Card holders must transfer their salary (the minimum monthly salary required is QR5,000) to QIB to be eligible or a fixed deposit of QR21,000. In this variation of an Islamic credit card, the monthly salary deposit acts like a fixed deposit during the term of the repayment. In August 2008, Bahrain Islamic Bank launched an Islamic Visa credit card structured much like other Islamic cards, with additional features such as the collection of loyalty points (air miles from Gulf Air).[42]

Muslim attitudes towards using bank cards vary from liberal to conservative, from disciplined use to unbridled spending. However, the vast majority of the global 1.5 billion Muslims have yet to have any card experience. In Pakistan, young women are increasingly using credit cards, counter to the traditional aversion to debt in South Asian markets. Unfortunately, there is a considerable gap in financial literacy in Muslim markets, with many customers falling into a debt spiral before learning how to manage the use of bank card products effectively. Fortunately, the influence of family members has played a significant role in shaping the attitudes of young card holders in Pakistan.

In the GCC markets, consumers are more knowledgeable about financial products than in other Muslim markets, and young consumers see Shariah-compliant credit cards as penalizing them for their beliefs, which has driven them towards prepaid cards. For example, a student using a conventional credit card with an annual subscription fee of 450 dirhams elects not to pay the balance in full at the end of the billing period and is assessed an interest charge of 100 dirhams. A second identical student using a Shariah-compliant card with the same card balance elects not pay the full amount of the balance, which results in a flat charge of 100 dirhams per month until the unpaid balance is paid, in addition to a monthly use fee of 150 dirhams per month. If the student using a conventional card repays the balance in 10 months, the total out-of-pocket charges including interest is 450 dirhams subscription + 100 dirhams × 10 months' interest = 1,450 dirhams in bank charges. The second student using the Shariah-compliant card with an identical balance repaying in 10 months incurs charges of 150 dirhams × 12 months' use or access fee + 100 dirhams x 10 months' flat penalty fee = 2,800 dirhams. In this scenario, the student using a Shariah-compliant card pays an additional financial penalty of 1,350 dirhams for practising their faith. Even customers who do not carry a balance have a perceived notion of an additional cost of 1,350 dirhams (1,800 dirhams monthly use fee for a Shariah-based card minus 450 dirhams for the annual conventional card fee) in order to practise Shariah compliancy in their bank card relationship (see Figure 2.3).

Islamic financial institutions must work diligently to align their charging mechanisms to compete directly with conventional banks, or invest in educating customers on the full utility of their products to justify the additional cost, or develop a clear and understandable value proposition.

Figure 2.3 Student Credit Card Comparison in the United Arab Emirates Market

Takaful

An oversimplification of *takaful* is to define it as Shariah-compliant insurance. In Arabic, *takaful* means "guaranteeing each other" – the principle of mutual assistance where risk is shared voluntarily by a group. In conventional terms, members of a group jointly agree to guarantee themselves against loss or damage to any of them as defined under the terms of a pact. Similar in construction to a conventional insurance policy, *takaful* involves an operator who accepts payment of instalments or contributions from participants of the plan, fund or scheme. The *takaful* contract reduces the uncertainty aspect of the plan or fund by having participants agree to relinquish as a gift a certain portion of their instalments. The contributions to the plan or fund are characteristically invested under the *mudarabah* principle and participants receive a predetermined share of the profit or loss of the investment pool. Typical uses of *takaful* are insuring property, vehicles, goods, valuables, health, accidents and life.

The number of *takaful* companies opening each year is steadily rising. In 2008, there were over 60 *takaful* companies operating in 23 countries. Worldwide *takaful* premiums are estimated to be in excess of US$2bn, representing roughly 9% of the global insurance market. Recent projections show that the industry could be worth as much as US$7.4bn by 2015. *Takaful* is not limited to Malaysia and the Middle East; in 2008, the Muang Thai Group formed a joint venture with the Islamic Bank of Thailand to offer Islamic insurance throughout Thailand.[43]

Perhaps one of the most progressive companies to enter the *takaful* market is Pakistan-based Pak-Qatar General Takaful, supported by Qatari organizations such as Qatar Islamic Insurance Company, Qatar International Islamic Bank, Qatar Islamic Bank, Qatar National Bank, the Amwal Group, Masraf Al Rayan and Munich-based FWU AG.

Mudarabah-based takaful

Common in Malaysia, the *mudarabah takaful* model demonstrates a clear distinction between the business of *takaful* or insurance and the business of investing funds mobilized from policy holders and/or shareholders. The *takaful* operator seeks no returns from managing the *takaful* business in line with the spirit of *takaful*, but seeks returns from the business of investing the *takaful* funds under a *mudarabah* agreement with the policy holders for managing their funds. The policy holders assume the role of fund provider or *rabb-al-maal* (capital owner). As a *mudarib* (agent or trustee), the *takaful* company receives its share of profits generated on investments (Figure 2.4).

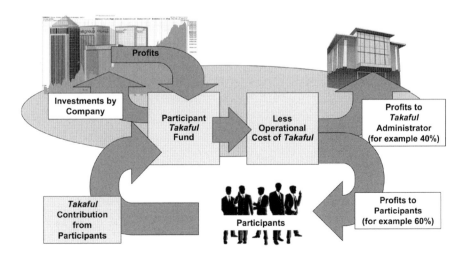

Figure 2.4 *Mudarabah Takaful* Model

Under the *mudarabah* model, profits generated by investments less operating costs are shared between the participants with a *takaful* operator. The sharing of such profits are based on prenegotiated ratios agreed to by the contracting parties. Generally, the structure of the *mudarabah* and its inherent risk sharing enables the *takaful* operator to share in the underwriting results from operations as well as the favourable performance returns on invested premiums. Losses are borne by the provider of capital. In the event of losses, the *mudarib* does not receive any compensation for his efforts. What is important to remember is that in a classical *mudarabah* contract, the *rabb al-mal* has no operational control over the project or investments.

Wakalah-based takaful

The *takaful* commonly found (although not exclusively) in the Middle East is the *wakalah*-based model, whereby the *takaful* operator acts as the *wakeel* or agent of the policy holders, and is compensated under a two-tier schedule whereby he is entitled to a known remuneration in addition to the incurrence of operational expenses on behalf of the principal (Figure 2.5). Agency fees are designed to offset operating costs and compensate and provide incentives for the *takaful* operator to ensure prudent underwriting, optimize investment performance, minimize direct operating expenses, minimize claims amount payable (thwart fraud), and ensure adequacy, equity and fairness between participants.

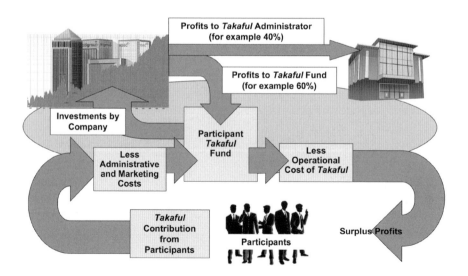

Figure 2.5 *Wakalah*-based *Takaful* Model

In March 2008, Noor Takaful was launched, funded by Noor Investment Group and Noor Islamic Bank. Using the *wakalah* model, Noor offers *takaful* insurance on a wide range of business and personal activities such as engineering/construction, motor vehicle, property, marine, general accident, liability, personal (mortgage, acci-care, credit shield, critical care and comprehensive care) and medical.[44]

Wakalah-waqf-based takaful
Some Shariah scholars have critically analysed the *wakalah* system and have suggested incorporating the concept of *waqf* into the *wakalah* model. Under this revised model, the operator would initially make a donation to establish a benevolent fund called the *waqf* fund. When this is created, the shareholders will lose their ownership rights on the *waqf*. However, this fund will be administered by the operator. The donations received from the participants seeking *takaful* protection will also be deposited into this fund and the combined amount will be used for investment. Profits earned will be deposited into the same fund. Participants will be given benefits from this *waqf* fund (Figure 2.6). The *waqf* fund would be allowed to form a contingency reserve fund apart from usual technical reserves. The *waqf* fund rules would define the basis for compensation and financial help, and rules for sharing surplus between the members and operators.

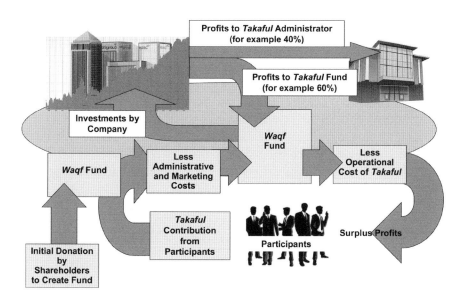

Figure 2.6 *Wakalah-waqf*-based *Takaful* model

Popular in Pakistan, the *wakalah-waqf* model establishes a relationship between the participants and the operator of the *waqf* fund. The operator, acting as the administrative agent of the fund, receives contributions from the participants to the *waqf* fund as a *tabarru* (donation, charity or gift). The contributions received are used for investment and the profits earned would again be deposited into the same fund, which also eliminates the issue of *gharar* (uncertainty).[45] Losses to the participant are paid by the company from the same fund. Operational expenses that are incurred by providing *takaful* services are also met from the same fund.

Shariah-compliant Derivatives

As Islamic finance enters the second generation of innovation, financing structures are becoming more sophisticated. As the first generation of Shariah-compliant products reaches market maturity, investors are looking for complementary derivatives products. The rise in investors' appetite for financial instruments with greater diversity creates an opportunity for derivatives practitioners to create new products. While market demand fuels new product design, it also creates new challenges for financial instruments that are conventionally designed for hedging and general risk management.

Malaysian banks have recognized that there are times when daily life creates conditions whereby a derivative-like feature can enhance a transaction still considered to be Shariah compliant. According to Norfadelizan bin Abd Rahman, head of product development at Bursa Malaysia, derivatives are judged to be Shariah compliant if they adhere to various structural components such as purpose, underlying asset, contract used, settlement method, image and the effect on the public and private parties involved.[46] In the Malaysian context, traditional Islamic contracts such as commodity *murabahah* or *musawamah* can be used when needed to fix prices and replicate conventional settlement methods, *bai salam* can be used as a forward pricing contract, *arbun* is applicable as an options contract, and *wa'ad* as a contract for flexibility.

Any discussion on Shariah-compliant derivates invites controversy because of the nature of the financial instrument when viewed through the constructs of divergent interpretations of Shariah principles, ranging from liberal to conservative in adherence to key ideals, on the speculative nature of derivative products. The fundamental Shariah requirements of certainty and transparency are contradicted by a forward dealing transaction. Some scholars argue that these transactions are varying degrees of speculation or gambling, which would make them prohibited. The basic premise of the forward contract is that the delivery of goods and payment are made on a future date, thus the uncertainty of the contract poses a potential loss to one of the two parties. This inequality in potential loss coupled with the uncertainty factor places the conventional deferred contract into an area of jeopardy under Shariah principles.

However, if these underlying breeches in Shariah principles can be mitigated by establishing clearer lines of equality on the duality of risk and return between the parties, then deferred obligations are permissible. For example, *bai muajjal* is a deferred payment on goods received right away, *bai salam/bai istisna* are payments made straightaway for goods to be delivered or manufactured over a period of time, and *arbun* comprises a payment of a deposit now, with the remaining balance to be paid in full upon delivery, whereby the deposit is forfeit should the contract is breached.

Our discussion turns briefly towards using *wa'ad* as a mechanism to satisfy Shariah principles for a forward-like contract. The *wa'ad* is a unilateral promise whereby both parties can choose to fulfil the obligation or not. Under a *wa'ad* agreement, specific details such as time of delivery, price, payment terms and the specific description of goods are not typically given a great deal of clarity, due to the underlying nature of the needs of each party. These built-in ambiguities make a *wa'ad* agreement appear to be flexible in construction, in that details are refined over time. The key differentiator is that the *wa'ad* agreement is an implied promise, not a contract. The *wa'ad* does have varying degrees of enforceability, however; Shariah scholars will take into account broader factors such as the fairness between parties and moral hazard. Under ideal conditions, a *wa'ad* agreement provides the flexibility for transactions that are now possible under modern economic conditions if constructed in a way that demonstrates equality between the parties. Theoretically, there is a downside to *wa'ad*; in the event of non-delivery by either party, a bias may be created that contradicts the original terms and conditions, placing one party at a clear disadvantage, thus, the fulfilment of the agreement may be settled via an arbiter who may rule in favour of one of the parties. The non-delivery may not be an intentional deception by either party, merely a change in the circumstances to which each party is subject to during the duration of the agreement.

Profit Rate Swaps

Based on *murabahah* (purchase and resale) contracts, a profit rate swap is similar to the conventional interest rate swap, whereby parties agree to exchange periodic fixed and floating payments by reference to a pre-agreed notional amount.[47] Uberoi observes that conventional interest rate swaps breach three fundamental tenets of Shariah law:

- the payment of interest

- uncertainty, since price, quantity or material characteristics of an asset sold may be subject to future payments linked to a floating rate

- speculation, as many futures and options contracts may be viewed in the same light as gambling.

Therefore, transactions must be structured so both parties benefit from positive risk sharing without violating one of these tenets. To be Shariah compliant, profit rate swaps use a single-term master *murabahah* contract that uses a series of fixed periodic payments dates. This type of reciprocal *murabahah* structure stipulates that under the terms of the sale, the financier purchases the goods from a supplier and resells them to a buyer at a marked-up price, with deferred payments. That is, there is a master agreement outlining the general exchange of goods with fixed payments, supplemented with a series of subordinate clauses (reverse *murabahah*) used to generate floating leg payments, whereby the cost/price is fixed while the profit rate is floating. The profit rate swap is simply an agreement to exchange profit/return/coupon rates between two counter-parties as a tool for hedging or asset liability management. Introduced by Bank Islam in Malaysia, the Wiqa Profit Rate Swap is an example of this type of product.[48]

Four Dimensions of Growth in Islamic Finance

Islamic finance has transcended borders and regions, but many challenges lie ahead before it can make that crucial leap from being an interesting but niche market to being an integral part of the global financial markets. Core deposits, loans, payment services and investments are at the heart of a successful retail bank. Customers value these services based on three basic criteria: rates, convenience and service quality. Banks lose customers when there is a significant weakness in any of these three areas, yet mere adequacy on the basics will not produce superior results. As the retail banking market for Shariah-compliant financial services changes over the next five years, an institution's success will increasingly depend on the quality and breadth of the total relationship with a customer. Islamic banks must demonstrate a superior service quality and a higher level of performance to grow a customer relationship from a single point of entry, like the opening of a bank account, into a durable, profitable, multifaceted relationship.

To meet the new competitive challenges in Islamic finance, Shariah-compliant banks must develop their competencies in CRM, lead management, cross-selling and retention. However, many banks have misdirected their efforts and have concentrated on retaining and expanding relationships with established customers. A higher return on capital is achievable when focusing resources on acquiring new customers and building customer confidence during the first few months of the relationship. Shariah-compliant institutions must focus their efforts on defining product packages to match offerings that are better suited to customer needs and encourage multifaceted relationships. Unlike other financial institutions whose deposit product packages are constructed on the basis of internal financial and production considerations, Islamic financial institutions must focus on the needs of prime customer segments.

Similar to conventional banking where there is a predisposition to direct new customers into a standardized blend of deposit-related products, including a current account, credit and/or debit cards, online banking and bill payment, Islamic banks must leverage their core banking products to achieve high cross-sell ratios. Although this approach often produces short-term results, it does little to build a long-term relationship, which is imperative for a competitive strategy. To compete in the changing Islamic financial marketplace, Islamic banks must differentiate themselves from larger international conventional competitors on the quality of service and not commoditized pricing. At the core of relationship building is an understanding of cross-selling, knowing when to apply products to specific customer needs. Customer retention is not achieved by increasing the number of products a customer has; rather, retention is proportional to the mix of products – ideally with at least one type of product relationship in each of the three domains: deposits, credit and investments.

Shariah-compliant product offerings must be targeted to particular customer segments and vary the profit rates, fees and minimum balance structures based on the total assets and liabilities that the customer brings to the institution – thus rewarding the overall value of the relationship. The key benchmark to success will be in measuring the annual customer attrition ratio, which needs to be less than 5%.

At the strategic level, Shariah-compliant product offerings must be tailored to meet the specific needs of particular customer segments. The big question for Islamic institutions is which specific needs in what segments will develop customer relationships while turning a profit for shareholders? To capitalize on market opportunities, a Shariah-compliant product mix must be flexible enough to be applied to a specific market segment and easily adjusted for application to other market segments.

Hence, innovation in Shariah-compliant finance plays a key role across four distinct areas of market growth: market breadth, length, quantity and depth, as illustrated in Figure 2.7. The strategic choices of financial institutions in this rapidly changing market are limited only by the availability of their resources. Smaller institutions will not have the financial resources to expand across all four dimensions simultaneously and in many cases will have to restrict their growth to one or two dimensions. Similarly, Shariah-compliant institutions operating in maturing Islamic finance markets, such as in Dubai, Doha and Manama, will focus on expansion into other markets versus new customer acquisition in their home markets.

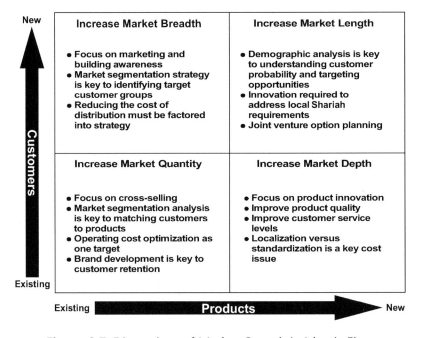

Figure 2.7 Dimensions of Market Growth in Islamic Finance

Fortunately, global economic conditions are creating many new opportunities for retail banks to develop new products and extend them to new customer segments. A Shariah-compliant retail bank's success will hinge on its ability to rapidly assess market opportunities and adapt its product mix to meet the specific needs of customers, regardless of segment. However, the universal rule for the relationship-building process is that all customer relationships must be constructed around a product mix, whereby the customer is enrolled in a three-account relationship that includes a deposit, loan (or line of credit) and an investment. The key objective in the relationship-building process is to facilitate the customer in building their wealth through deposits and investments while enabling a customer to build a credit history.

With these customer objectives in mind, each market opportunity for a Shariah-compliant bank must be able to enhance the customer relationship by offering a way to build a customer's deposits, financing or investments.

Product Saturation (Existing Products to Existing Customers)

Although it is unfair to generalize, most Shariah-compliant banks compete purely for market share, selling the same products to the same customers. In Shariah-compliant finance and Islamic retail banking around the world, the primary focus is on large corporate financing activities or customers in the upper third of the economic pyramid. The strategic endgame for Shariah-compliant banks in this context is clear – customer retention and product saturation (or cross-selling). Innovation occurs along two distinct lines: a determined focus on improving the quality of service, and the repackaging or repurposing of existing products to appeal to existing customers. When banks engage in a process of innovation applied to these two strategic variables, the result is organic growth or an improvement in top-line performance.

The first strategic step is to improve the quality of service, which is proportional to the retention rate of customers. To improve customer service, Shariah-compliant banks must first know their customers through the process of customer profiling and market segmentation. Muslims (like all other customer groups) have a variety of lifestyles, with a wide range of financial requirements. Aligning products to specific market segments is one part of the equation; meanwhile an institution must also assess and set service levels that equate directly to specific market segments. Once market segments are clearly defined and service levels set, Shariah-compliant institutions must then address the overall quality of service in the context of brand representation. Branding in Islamic finance is paramount to customers identifying with the products and services of the bank. When repackaging existing products into new offerings, how the new product is positioned, and subsequently sold to the target market segment, is determined by the brand identity of the product, reinforced by the integrity of the institution.

One example of effective cross-selling of Shariah-compliant services is the collaboration between Bank Islam Malaysia and Lembaga Tabung Haji (the Pilgrim's fund), a savings schema for *hajj* pilgrims. Tabung Haji's depositors gain access to Shariah-compliant banking products, such as home financing and Bank Islam cards, and customize services for pilgrims. Bank Islam has targeted a rise of 25% in consumer banking revenues as the benchmark for this cross-selling relationship from 5.1 million Tabung Haji depositors (RM12.8bn total accumulated savings).[49] Linking complementary service to a specific market segment or specialized customer behaviour such as a pilgrimage is key to cross-selling Shariah-compliant services.

The second strategic step is to manage proactively the relationship with the customer by monitoring communications to avoid offering too many additional products too soon. Confusing or overwhelming customers with offers often alienates them. Privacy issues are a rising concern with customers as banks begin to offer products from partners or third party providers. Cross-sell ratios at conventional European banks average between 2.3 and 5.5 products per customer (Spain's BBVA Group reports 4.5 products per customer), while ratios in US banks remain slightly higher, with Wells Fargo reporting a cross-sell ratio of 5.73 products per customer in 2008.[50] In Shariah-compliant banks and conventional banks in emerging markets, the ratio is often lower, for example in India, ICICI Bank's cross-sell ratio is 1.1 products per customer.[51]

Product Proliferation (New Products to Existing Customers)

One key strategy is to plant the perception of trading up, moving towards more sophisticated products, which in turn (and theoretically) will yield a better deal for the customer. New products offered to existing customers must meet one of two criteria: they offer a new or unique capability that was previously unknown to the customer or the product must be seen as significantly superior (or a premium) to existing products. New products can be marketed or packaged in several ways to engage existing customers, such as offering complementary products that add to an existing relationship, for example customers with savings accounts might be encouraged to take an additional account to save for a specific item or event (wedding, *hajj* or education).

Bank collaborations with financial software vendors often fail when they do not have a clear value proposition for a specific customer market segment. For example, smart cards and electronic cash systems have had little success in US markets because customers cannot determine their value to them. Conversely, electronic money systems such as M-Pesa in Kenya are extremely popular because they facilitate payments and money transfers without having to own a bank account. Similarly, Hong Kong's Octopus card and London's Barclays Oyster card enable users to ride public transport without having to buy tickets, making commuting easier.

The key to selling new products to existing customers is to develop products that customers want through a process of listening to customers and creating an effective marketing/brand strategy. Specific product characteristics must resonate with targeted customer behaviours within a narrowly defined market segment. Customer retention is the prime measure of a successful strategy. When banks innovate new products to existing customers, the goal is customer retention. Operationally, to sell new products and services to bank customers, financial services companies must move from an order-taking culture to a sales relationship culture.

One of the prime rules of banking is the realization that it takes far more effort to win new customers than it does to service existing ones. In banking, the cost of customer acquisition is high, so once a customer relationship is won, the focus should shift to keeping that customer. Customer satisfaction is paramount; in numerous cases, high-quality service and superior customer handling skills are often more important that product pricing with many customer segments. Well-trained staff are essential in generating customer loyalty. Although many banks believe that discounts and special deals for premium customers retain customers and encourage customers to use additional banking products, nothing is more effective than superior customer service to build a loyal customer base.

Another strategy is to introduce third party products to existing customers, such as insurance, or other ancillary services. In June 2008, Alliance Islamic Bank, Malaysia introduced Alliance Fixed Investment-i (AFI), a new Islamic fixed deposit product under a joint venture with Okachi Malaysia, which uses commodities traded under the Tokyo Grain Exchange and Central Japan Commodity Exchange for deposit placement.[52] The AFI account, based on the *tawarruq* concept, is targeted at large corporate depositors looking for a fixed return that is determined upfront. Alliance Islamic Bank's strategy is to grow its market share by promoting Islamic financial products and capitalizing on existing conventional banking customers and distribution channels. The strategy is to integrate third party products into Alliance Islamic Bank's product portfolio to improve the bank's liquidity position while improving its financing–deposit ratio. Regardless of the strategic approach to selling new products to existing customers, the intention is to increase the number of customer choices and enhance customer experience by providing products that fulfil various aspects of their lifestyle.

Customer Acquisition (Existing Products to New Customers)

The acquisition of customers, or market penetration, involves selling more of your current products to new customers within targeted market segments. Shariah-compliant financial institutions must develop strategies that address the consumer appetites of Muslims and non-Muslims. Penetrating Muslim consumer markets used to be a process of simply appealing to the religious aspect of Islamic banking. Now, however, consumers are becoming more sophisticated, demanding more diversity in products with increased convenience. Banks and non-bank entities offering Shariah-compliant financial products must now shift their focus to developing stronger local/national/regional brand identities. To cater to non-Muslim customers, Islamic banks are emphasizing the ethical/moral aspect of their product offerings.

The lesson learned by financial services companies trying to sell banking services to new customers is that to successfully penetrate a new customer segment you must invest heavily in understanding your customer. Market research into the specific wants, desires, needs and aspirations of customers reveals a litany of characteristics that drive their financial behaviour. People in all market segments have fundamentally different attitudes towards savings and spending, often prioritizing their needs for payment services, investments and financing needs in vastly different ways.

In numerous markets for Shariah-based financial services, the concentration of bank offerings has been primarily to cater to people in the banked upper third of the population. In January 2009, the Bank of London and The Middle East (BLME) extended its wealth management division, launching a Shariah-compliant private banking business for high net worth customers.[53] As the markets for Shariah-compliant finance mature, more institutions will change their focus towards the working middle class and the focus must switch to cost leadership and price performance. To extend products into new customer segments, banks are developing three strategies: expanding market presence, franchising products to other distribution channels, and developing aggressive marketing campaigns. Just as in conventional banking, additional locations offer customers convenient access to services. Convenience is increasingly becoming a valued commodity among young Muslims as career and family demand more of their time. Within the Middle East and Africa, many nations are reporting up to 50% of their populations as being under 30, from which we can extrapolate that access and convenient service from all delivery channels must be on the strategic agenda for Shariah-compliant banks. Franchising financial services is another option for Shariah-compliant institutions; however, unlike their conventional counterparts, the institution must ensure that the franchisee maintains strict adherence to Shariah principles.

Marketing is building awareness for an institution's products and services to a general consumer/business base or to specific market segments. Branding, on the other hand, is a representation of the sum of experiences over time between an individual and the institution, financial service or banking product. Shariah-compliant institutions must build and reinforce their brands not simply to broadcast their product offerings but to set the expectations of customers as to the level of quality of service and the degree of trust. Islamic financial institutions are initiating a redefinition of their brands as they try to appeal to additional Muslim demographic segments and non-Muslims.

Market Expansion (New Products to New Customers)

Geographic diversification is one strategy for Shariah-compliant banks that gives an institution the ability to offer new products not currently in demand to a local populace. Islamic banks and non-banks offering Shariah-based financing realize that institutional growth provides an opportunity to spread fixed costs over a larger asset base, reducing the unit costs of the institution while supporting an increased return on assets. Expanding the asset base across multiple geographies creates an opportunity to increase revenue by capturing market share in other markets. Historically, this process is difficult as a new market entrant (a foreign institution) must compete against local institutions for an initial small market share and then work diligently to expand its market presence. However, in the Islamic finance industry, the opposite applies, as so few Shariah-compliant financial products exist in Muslim countries that sheer lack of services enables market expansion with little initial competitive pressure in numerous emerging markets. However, even though the competitive pressure might be less than in the saturated banking markets, Shariah-compliant banks must also be aware that there is still increased pressure for performance as assets increase. New markets also introduce an additional risk factor on lending/financing decisions, as local knowledge is often required to substantiate credit histories and customer backgrounds.

The greatest opportunity for innovation in Islamic finance is to move into emerging markets because there are millions of customers requiring banking services of any kind. In many markets, customers (businesses and consumers) often do not understand Islamic finance, even if they are Muslim. Thus, the Islamic bank may need to fill more of an educator role than usual. This may mean spending more time with customers to explain available products, conducting customized workshops or helping to complete forms. Additionally, management many need to hire know-ledgeable lenders, sales reps and managers who have experience with the banking services offered and the clientele.

Regardless of the market, moving into new markets provides a new range of opportunities for Shariah-compliant institutions to hedge their future profitability by spreading their services across multiple national economies. Economic diversity enables Islamic financial institutions to concentrate their efforts against the economic trends within a single nation that is experiencing growth, while reducing or realigning services in national economies that are experiencing cyclical declines.

For example, in June 2008, Noor Islamic Bank expanded services to Tunisia as its first foray into a new market offering investment and corporate banking services.[54] In April 2008, the BLME participated in a US$20m forward lease financing to Qatar Electricity and Water Company for the construction of a water desalination plant.[55] The Islamic Bank of Thailand plans on expanding its branch network from 26 to 56.[56] Bahrain-based Al Baraka Islamic Bank has also put forward a campaign to convert itself into a local bank in Pakistan and invest US$80m to expand its network from 12 to 30 branches.[57] And Qatari-based Masraf Al Rayan bank established a clear two-tier expansion strategy, launching new branches in Qatar and expanding its market presence into Libya.[58]

Notes

1   Schoon, N. (2007) Islamic finance: expansion brings challenges, *Professional Investor*, February.

2   *Rules for Branch Managers*, Lloyds Banking Company Ltd, December, 1874, pp. 4–5.

3   *Rules for Branch Managers*, Lloyds Banking Company Ltd, December, 1874, p. 11.

4   Tahir, S. (2003) *Future of Islamic Banking*, International Islamic University (Islamabad), discussion paper, March, pp. 7–8.

5   The following banks did not provide details of their financial statements and have been excluded from this analysis: HSBC Amanah, US$15.194bn, Bank Maskan Iran (Housing Bank), US$13.075bn, Bank Sanat Va Madan (Bank of Industry and Mines), US$3.792bn, Bank Islam Brunei Darussalam, US$2.723bn.

6   Solé, J. (2007) Introducing Islamic banking into conventional banking systems, IMF Working Paper, WP/07/175, July, p. 20.

7   Islamic Interbank Money Market, www.iimm.bnm.gov.my.

8   Liquidity Management Centre, www.lmcbahrain.com.

9   Bursa Malaysia (2008) Innovation: driving the future of Malaysia's Islamic capital market, *Islamic Finance Asia*, August/September, p. 51.

10 Henry, P.B. (2003) Commentary on Bekaert, Harvey and Lundblad's "Equity market liberalization in emerging equity markets", Stanford University, Research Paper No. 1783, February, p. 6.

11 Bursa Malaysia (2008) Innovation: driving the future of Malaysia's Islamic capital market, *Islamic Finance Asia*, August/September, p. 52.

12 Ahmed Moola, Head of Islamic Banking at ABSA, interview with the authors, October, 2008.

13 Ebrahim Fayez Al Shamsi, CEO Emirates Islamic Bank, interview with the authors, October, 2008.

14 Ebrahim Fayez Al Shamsi, CEO, Emirates Islamic Bank, interview with the authors, October, 2008.

15 Al Salam Bank, Time deposit (wakala), www.alsalambahrain.com/wakala.aspx.

16 Wakala Treasury Deposit Account, Islamic Bank of Britain, April, 2008, www.islamic-bank.com/islamicbanklive/WakalaTreasuryDepositAccount/1/Home/1/Home.jsp.

17 Investment deposit account (wakala investment), Boubyan Bank, January, 2009, www.bankboubyan.com/deposit_account.htm.

18 Retail savings accounts, Bosna Bank International, www.bbi.ba.

19 Johara Banking, Dubai Islamic Bank, www.alislami.ae/en/joharabanking.htm.

20 'Ladies only' credit card recognises needs of financially independent women, corporate press release, First Gulf Bank, September 17, 2006, www.fgb.ae/en/aboutus/presskit/ladiescard.asp.

21 Ranzini, S.L., University Bank, interview with the authors, 2008.

22 Brandenburger, A. and Nalebuff, B. (1996) *Co-Opetition: A Revolution Mindset that Combines Competition and Cooperation*.

23 Booming Islamic bond market embroiled in debate over religious compliance, *International Herald Tribune*, January 11, 2008.

24 Roane, K.R. (2008) Fatally flawed bonds, Bloomberg, September 23.

25 *Sukuk* Shari'ah compliance an issue, CPI Financial, January 26, 2009, www.cpifinancial.net.

26 Damak, M., Volland, E. and Maheshwari, R. (2009) *Sukuk* issuance fell dramatically in 2008 but long-term market prospects are good, Standard and Poor's Rating Direct Report, January 14, p. 2.

27 Jobst, A., Kunzel, P., Mills, P. and Sy, A. (2008) Islamic bond issuance: what sovereign debt managers need to know, IMF Policy Discussion Paper (PDP/08/03), July, p. 3.

28 Maronese, L., director, group corporate communications, Ithmaar Banking Group, interview with the authors, October, 2008.

29 Hesse, H., Jobst, A. and Sole, J. (2008) Current trends in Islamic structured finance and capital markets, IMF, September 2.

30 Alvi, Ijlal, Capacity building needs of issuing sovereign sukuk, International Islamic Financial Market (IIFM), p. 2, www.djindexes.com/mdsidx/downloads/Islamic/articles/capacity-building.pdf.

31 Wilson, R. (2005) Overview of the sukuk market, Islamic bonds: your guide to issuing, structuring and investing in sukuk, *Euromoney*, p. 9.

32 Alvi, Ijlal, Capacity building needs of issuing sovereign sukuk, International Islamic Financial Market (IIFM), p. 2, www.djindexes.com/mdsidx/downloads/Islamic/articles/capacity-building.pdf.

33 Brunei sells $165 million worth of sukuk, *The Brunei Times*, April 3, 2009, www.bt.com.bn.

34 Bank Islam Card-i: Pre-paid card, Bank Islam, February 15, 2009, www.bankislam.com.my/Pre-paid_Card.aspx.

35 Jeans Card, Sharjah Islamic Bank, press release July 29, 2008, www.sib.ae/en/news/.

36 UK's first Islamic prepaid card hits the market, *New Horizon*, 29 August, 2008, www.newhorizon-islamicbanking.com.

37 Hajj and Umra Card, Kuwait Finance House, January 14, 2009, www.kfh.com.

38 Launching zakat affinity card, corporate press release, Lebanese Islamic Bank, September 18, 2008, www.lebaneseislamicbank.com.lb/newsinformation.asp?id=10.

39 Wilson, R., Parallels between Islamic and ethical banking, pp. 11–12, www.sc.com.my/html/iaffairs/ioscoislamicpdf/Parallels.pdf.

40 EONCAP Islamic Debit MasterCard, EONCAP Islamic Bank Berhad, 2008, www.eoncap-islamicbank.com.my.

41 Bankernet Card, Lebanese Islamic Bank, February 2, 2009, www.lebaneseislamicbank.com.lb.

42 Bahrain Islamic bank launches new visa credit card, August 16, 2008, http://zawya.com/story.cfm/sidZAWYA20080816112727/.

43 Chudasri, D. (2008) Muang Thai to offer Islamic insurance, *Bangkok Post*, September 26, www.bangkokpost.com.

44 Noor Takaful, product offerings, www.noortakaful.com

45 Takaful models, Academy for International Modern Studies, Islamic Banking & Finance, Online Certification definitions, p.1.

46 Rahman, Norfadelizan bid Abd (2008) Commodity murabahah: as a basic foundation of Islamic derivate & structured product, presentation to the Malaysian Structured Product Forum 2008, Bursa Malaysia Bhd, May 29, p. 3.

47 Uberoi, P. (2009) Profit rate swap, Allen & Overy, White Paper, p. 2, www.allenovery.com/AOWeb/binaries/47753.PDF.

48 Wiqa profit rate swap, Bank Islam, February 10, 2009, www.bankislam.com.my/Wiqa_Profit_Rate_Swap.aspx.

49 Bank Islam taps Tabung Haji synergy, Bank Islam Malaysia, corporate archives, www.bankislam.com.my.

50 Wells Fargo gets personal, *Retail Banker International*, February 9, 2009, p. 17.

51 ICICI bank to focus on cross-selling retail products, *Financial Express*, June 14, 2006, www.financialexpress.com/news/.

52 Alliance Islamic Bank launches first Islamic fixed deposit product, Alliance Islamic Bank, press release, June 9, 2008, www.allianceislamicbank.com.my/pressreleases_2008_090608.html.

53 BLME moves into the Shari'ah-compliant private banking business, CPI Financial, January 22, 2009, www.cpifinancial.net.

54 Noor Islamic Bank opens office in Tunisia, CPI Financial, June 22, 2008, www.cpifinancial.net.

55 Bank of London and the Middle East participates in Qatar infrastructure financing, CPI Financial, April 8, 2008, www.cpifinancial.net.

56 Y-Sing, L. and Li Lian, L. (2009) Sharia harmonisation possible in long run, Thai Bank, Arabian Business.com, March 2, www.arabianbusiness.com/.

57 Al Baraka Islamic Bank to invest $80m on Pakistan expansion, Dow Jones Newswires, April 18, 2008.

58 Masraf Al Rayan, TAIB Research: Research Report, March 5, 2009, p. 1.

3

EMERGING FINANCIAL HUBS

Industry discussions on Islamic financial innovation typically concentrate on two features: technology and new banking products. The application of technology by an institution or the creation of financial products is easy to discuss because they are tangible parts of an industry-wide process. The development of products that cater to a specific lifestyle need is measurable; consumers either use them or they do not. When an institution uses a financial product to address a specific socioeconomic problem such as banking for the poor, the results are observed and measured. One aspect of innovation that is often absent from mainstream discussions is Islamic financial innovation on a macroeconomic scale. The rise of Islamic finance has precipitated the establishment of new financial centres throughout the Middle East and Asia.

Innovation in Islamic finance is now taking place on the world theatre on a grand scale. It is important to consider the rise of these new financial centres in the context of total market development and as a continual process of innovation, as each financial centre strives to specialize in one or more aspects of Islamic finance. Just as multinational corporations establish operating departments to expand their product lines, create new manufacturing capacity or move into new business lines to diversify their product mix, so the rise of new financial centres acts to broaden the access to Shariah-compliant services as well as spread business risks over an increased number of national economies. Increasing access to Islamic banking services is a common theme among banks operating in the Gulf Cooperation Council (GCC), such as Dubai Islamic Bank's domestic expansion plans to open 10 new branches and increase the customer base by 15% during 2009[1] and international expansion plans such as Noor Islamic Bank's into Tunisia.

What is driving the growth in the markets for Shariah-compliant banking services? An analysis of the markets reveals a misalignment between the current Islamic financial capabilities and the centres of Muslim populations. Countries benefiting from oil revenues have been creating new capacity in Shariah-compliant institutions that have been focused on serving local populations primarily in Malaysia and the Middle East. The mismatch of market capacity indicates a greater need for innovation and economic integration on the most basic economic activities such as commercial banking, migrant remittances and transnational trade. Market alignment will come from two sources: the expansion of existing financial institutions into Muslim populations where Shariah-compliant financial services are lacking, and new institutions. Innovation will come from four strategic initiatives: technology to increase access, new products, rethinking institutional internal processes, and new forms of joint ventures.

An examination of the distribution of Shariah-based banking services worldwide shows that although the Islamic finance industry is growing, the majority of the capabilities of the industry are not located in nations with dense Muslim populations, as shown in Figure 3.1.

However, when the capacity for Islamic finance is contrasted against the distribution of Muslim populations worldwide, shown in Figure 3.2, one can see that there is a clear mismatch between Islamic financial capacity and serviceable populations. The mismatch in industry capacity and Muslim populations can be attributed largely to three primary factors: the infancy of the industry, a shortage of financial technological infrastructures throughout the regions, and a lack of access to banking services for local populations.

We can see that the distribution of financial services is one aspect of Islamic finance in dire need of innovation. The inherently risk-adverse nature of Islamic finance mangers may act to impede innovation in distribution networks due the amount of investment needed with no clear return on investment. When this same dilemma is seen in conventional banks, risk-adverse institutions are rarely market leaders.

The Potential for Additional Growth

The growth potential of Islamic finance has not gone unnoticed by western markets, as London has made significant investments to establish itself as a centre for Shariah-compliant financial services. The rising interest in developing financial hubs throughout the Middle East and other Muslim nations is not simply to consolidate Islamic financial activities but to stimulate more efficient cross-border capital flows and econ-

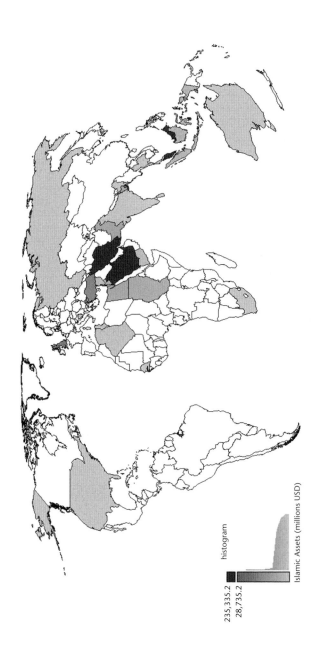

histogram

235,335.2
28,735.2

Islamic Assets (millions USD)

Figure 3.1 Assets of Banks Offering Shariah-compliant Services, 2008

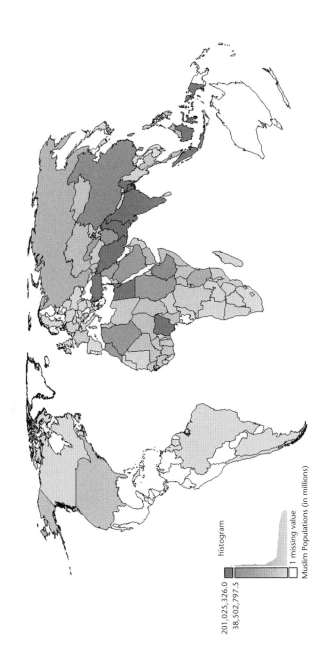

Figure 3.2 Distribution of Worldwide Muslim Population

Source: Maris Strategies

histogram

201,025,326.0

38,502,797.5

1 missing value

Muslim Populations (in millions)

omic liberalization. Islamic financial innovations are diversifying their respective markets; however, if taken in the context of the Islamic finance industry, these innovations are acting to strengthen and enlarge emerging markets, which in turn will cushion local economies from asymmetric economic shocks. To avoid overreaction in the financial markets, these hubs are concentrating on promoting the adoption of transnational risk management standards and other efforts to synchronize regional monetary policy.

The financial events of 2008–09 on the world stage reacquaint us with the risks of cavalier capitalism where overleveraging and reckless off-balance sheet transactions are overlooked in the pursuit of ever bigger returns on investment. What bankers, governments and consumers have learned is that financial leverage is two-way street as small structural weaknesses in local regulatory regimes become compound problems as transnational finance acts to feed on itself. Thus, overleveraging, structural weaknesses and an excess in consumption by industrialized nations have set the stage for a realignment of the control mechanisms for financial activities around the world. One aspect of global socioeconomics that has not been factored into the financial reorganization is to redress the imbalance of global financial inequalities. Notwithstanding this, Islamic finance is not a cure for all the woes of world financial markets; however, the Islamic financial industry is in a position to provide a model framework to address a number of global socioeconomic challenges. It is because the Islamic financial industry is in its adolescence that industry leaders, comprising bankers, central bankers, politicians and policy makers, can learn from the mistakes of their western counterparts and develop oversight mechanisms, which endeavour to ensure a higher quality of financial trustworthiness.

Several factors have made significant contributions to maintaining the fidelity of Islamic finance found in the main tenets of Shariah law, namely the overarching concept of sharing risk and returns. As the Islamic finance industry matures and transaction levels rise, a growing body of evidence confirms that Shariah-compliant institutions take a conservative posture when managing risks that are shared with their customers. Another factor that influences an institution's risk management philosophy is that Shariah-compliant transactions are backed by tangible assets, not simply securitized debt obligations or other instruments not represented by a physical asset such as a building, land or commodities. These factors, coupled with adequate market and institutional safeguards, set the stage for institutions to manage risks with a rigour that strengthens the quality of capital employed. Thus, the development of financial centres throughout the Muslim world is laying the foundation for a financial system that will serve the financial requirements of Muslims, while offering an alternative financial system to conventional investors, consumers and business.

Building Economic Capitals

Middle Eastern and Asian cities such as Doha, Dubai, Manama, Kuala Lumpur, Riyadh, and many others are vying to become financial gateways to Muslim populations across the globe. In Saudi Arabia, new financial centres are under construction or are in the final stages of planning. Among the attempts to increase awareness of Islamic finance is the creation of international and local financial hubs, including the Dubai International Financial Centre and Business Bay, Dubai Multi Commodities Centre, Bahrain Financial Harbour, Ras Al Khaimah Financial City, King Abdullah Economic City, Barwa Financial District, Qatar Financial Centre, and the Malaysia International Islamic Financial Centre. These financial hubs have different visions for the future of Shariah-compliant finance in the different regions of the globe. In the context of Islamic innovation, the goal is not the mainstream acceptance of Islamic finance by world markets, or to make Islamic finance all-encompassing, rather the objective is to provide a suite of financial tools to Muslims on a global scale.

It is clear that the overall expansion of the industry is not limited to Islamic nation states, as the demand for Islamic banking is increasing in non-Muslim countries as well. For example, in Kenya, a predominately non-Muslim state, Islamic banks are reporting that as many as 20% of their customers are non-Muslims. The strategy that banks are using for their initial foray into non-Muslim markets is to construct products in such a way that Muslims can compare Islamic banking offerings with their interest-bearing conventional counterparts. Banks of all sizes are offering some form of Shariah-compliant product, from international giants like HSBC Amanah, Standard Chartered Saadiq, Lloyds TSB, Citigroup, Deutsche Bank, JP Morgan, Lehman Brothers and UBS to smaller specialized institutions like the Islamic Bank of Britain, University Islamic Financial, American Finance House LARIBA, and Devon Bank, Chicago. Recently in the USA, institutions like Freddie Mac and Fannie Mae have purchased mortgages from several non-bank mortgage finance companies that offer Shariah-compliant products (unfortunately, to qualify for loans under these schemes, in many cases a borrower must purchase private mortgage insurance that may not be Shariah compliant). GCC-based banks are also moving into external markets such as Bahrain-based First Islamic Investment Bank, which operates a subsidiary in Atlanta, Georgia, offering direct investment, real estate and asset management services.

In terms of innovation in asset management services, for example, Douglas Clark Johnson, CEO and chief investment strategist at Calyx Financial, stated that:

> The biggest challenge facing the Islamic asset management business is building in-house talent and capabilities to broaden and deepen the array of products available for portfolio allocation purposes, not looking to legitimize "financial engineering" in a Shariah-compliant context. It is the difference between horizontal and vertical evolution. The fact that so many Islamic funds are sub-advised [represented by back and forth discussions between Shariah scholars and investment managers on the degrees of compliance or the local idiosyncrasies of Shariah interpretation] back to established conventional managers has meant that the Islamic business has become an investment strategy taker, rather than an investment strategy giver. A list of secular themes from which a portfolio of funds might evolve include cultural demonstration across the Muslim world, the development of agribusinesses for food security, especially in the Middle East, rural empowerment through microfinance and other initiatives. Granted, some of these concepts overlap with themes we see elsewhere in the developing world, while others might be uniquely relevant to Shariah-sensitive investors.

The Market Potential Beyond the Middle East

So what is the potential market for Islamic banking outside the Middle East? If we look at the Americas and Europe, the initial market potential is obviously the 60.2 million Muslims and perhaps an additional 5 million non-Muslims who are looking for alternative investments:

- The Americas – 10.2 million people (6.3 million in the USA alone, the remainder spread across Brazil, Canada, Argentina, Mexico, Panama, Honduras, Trinidad and Tobago, Guyana, Venezuela, Surinam and Columbia in descending order of population).

- Europe – 50 million people (Russia 27 million, France 6.1, Germany 3 million, Bosnia-Herzegovina 2.3, Albania 2.2, Serbia and Montenegro 2 million, UK 1.5 million and the rest distributed across the European continent).

The difficulty in serving these markets is the dispersion of Muslims across these geographical locations. Fortunately, the majority of Muslims are typically found in urban areas. In addition, there is a potential of approximately 5 million non-Muslims who are latent customers in these markets.

In the USA, providing Islamic banking and financial services is more complex than in other nations because the responsibility for regulatory supervision is divided between a number of federal and state agencies. The regulatory structure of the US market poses distinctly different challenges for Islamic banking such as the treatment of profit and loss-sharing deposit accounts, the types of permissible investments commercial banks can hold, and various disclosure requirements (for example the advance disclosure of annual percentage rates to comply with the Truth in Lending Act 1968). To limit banks from assuming unnecessary risks, the US regulatory structure (concerning deposit activity) limits the range of investments that a commercial bank can be engaged in, typically fixed income, interest-bearing securities. Although limits like these are designed primarily to limit potential losses to depositors, they create a challenge for banks trying to comply with Shariah principles. However, institutions like University Islamic Financial Corp. have designed products that comply with the regulatory conditions such as profit-sharing deposits that are insured by the Federal Deposit Insurance Corporation. Perhaps one of the most challenging issues for Islamic finance in the USA is financing the purchase of a home or car using *murabahah* or *ijarah* structures, where under some state laws, the institution may be required to qualify as a licensed leasing company.

The key issue is that bank supervisors must develop a new understanding of how risk is managed under the distinctive structure of an Islamic bank, and to assess the safety and soundness of an Islamic institution in a way that fairly evaluates the approach used in matters such as credit risk, investment risk, operational risk, compliance, corporate governance and capital policy. That said, US regulators are quickly learning the fundamentals of how to address these regulatory issues in ways that make Islamic banking more inclusive to their markets. The US Department of Treasury now has an Islamic scholar in residence to address specifically the issues of Islamic banking and finance.

However, providing Shariah-compliant services in the USA is not new, as organizations such as Saturna Capital Corp. entered the market in 1986 with the Amana Income Fund, which was followed in 1994 with the Amana Growth Fund. Now under new management and with $25m, Saturna Capital has operations in Washington state, Virginia and New York.

Perhaps one key issue in non-Muslim markets is the attraction of

Islamic banking and finance to non-Muslims who are beginning to equate compliance with Shariah principles as synergistic with ethical and socially responsible investing. Interestingly, the most compatible customers and investors are devout Christians who seek alternative investments that are free from supporting industries such as pornography and gambling. Many of the underlying principle investment strategies and objectives in the Ave Maria Catholic Values Fund are strikingly similar to those of similar Islamic alternatives.

Some key developments of non-Middle Eastern banks in terms of Islamic banking in 2006 include the UK's Lloyds TSB's Shariah-compliant banking, Deutsche Bank's Islamic window and *sukuk* securities, Dow Jones and Citigroup Corporate and Investment Bank's launch of the Dow Jones Citigroup Sukuk Index and the UK's Islamic Bank of Britain's opening of a new branch in Birmingham. The increase in offerings of Islamic banking in non-Muslim countries and the profits shown so far by these endeavours reveal that banks are right to be enthusiastic about entering this new market.

The New Economic Centres and Hubs

Governments in emerging economies are rapidly understanding the role of financial infrastructure development and the use of finance and banking as a direct means to stimulate economic development. In most cases, this development is emerging as a collaboration of public/private partnerships whereby the government's role is to create a vision of the future and provide the necessary funding to set the process of development in motion. Once development has begun, periodic injections of investment are needed to maintain forward momentum towards the vision. Again, innovation is playing a substantial role in the process of development. Governments have come to realize that they must act to create the catalyst for economic development and provide enough flexibility in legal, trade and regulatory frameworks to accommodate innovation. That is not to say that governments are not adequately regulating economic, financial and banking activities; rather, governments are learning that market innovation must come first followed by a continual revision of regulations, trade agreements and other frameworks to accommodate the results of an innovative process.

One such innovation is the establishment of new financial centres to promote economic development. Throughout the Muslim world, governments are launching plans for new hubs of finance to act as a gateway to their market and markets in adjacent nations. The early activities of these centres have focused on big business activities such as financing building construction, capital markets development, infrastructure projects and commodity trading. As these centres mature with increased volumes and the introduction of a wider array of financial instruments, the next stage of their development is to act as a platform for local and transnational small business activities and to encourage the movement of economic activity from the informal sector to the formal economy. During the past five years, several economic cities have emerged or their foundations have been put in place, as shown in Figure 3.3.

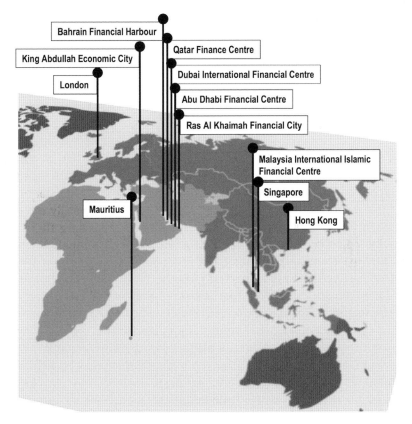

Figure 3.3 Emerging Financial Hubs

Dubai

For over a decade now, Dubai has been marketing itself as a natural financial hub in the Middle East. Political and economic stability, coupled with government policies aimed at fostering economic diversification and liberalization, has created a safe and secure business environment for the United Arab Emirates (UAE), a nation built on immigrants from many nations. Dubai has learned that infrastructure starting with a modern telecommunication network enables citizens to participate in the global economy. Dubai's high internet penetration (28% in Dubai versus 17% in the Middle East and North Africa, including 1.5 million mobile phone users for a population of 2.5 million) illustrates that consumption rises proportionately with the availability of infrastructure capacity. Put simply, as additional telecommunications infrastructure is made available, consumers and business will use the added capacity. Several reasons explain this phenomenon: a extraordinary number of professional and technology workers living or moving to Dubai, the age of the working population (like many Middle Eastern nations, the vast majority of citizens are under 30), and a transportation infrastructure that enables businesses to use Dubai as a hub throughout the Middle East, Africa, Southern Asia and Eastern Europe.

Dubai's strategy for economic diversification hinges on the "free zones", that is, designated areas where firms in a specific sector operate under a special legal and regulatory regime that complies with international standards and best practices. The free zones are quite separate from the UAE's legal system, and they offer a more business-friendly environment to foreign investors. In Dubai, 27 free zones, including the Dubai International Financial Centre (DIFC), are already operational and more are in the pipeline. An important part of Dubai's 2015 economic plan is the expectation that the banking and financial sector will contribute up to 15.1% of GDP. For the DIFC, the vision is that it will shape tomorrow's financial map as a global gateway for capital and investment, acting as an internationally accepted common law legal framework, a regulated financial centre with full transparency, a platform to centralize regional wealth for economic growth and development, a channel for new wealth and a link to the international markets.

The DIFC's understanding of Islamic finance centres on an underlying belief that the regulation of Islamic finance and conventional finance should be closely aligned. In its view, the DIFC's role as a regulator is to focus its efforts on the adequacy of the systems and controls that financial services providers use to maintain their compliance obligations. The DIFC has elected not to regulate the religious features of Islamic products, but rather to ensure that those features are addressed by others under adequate systems and controls.[4]

At the current level of market maturity, Islamic finance needs an organization that will act as a collaborative hub for the coordination of regional regulatory standards. The Dubai Financial Services Authority (DFSA) is working with regional and international regulatory bodies and entering into cooperative and information-sharing arrangements with other regulators and counterparties. The DFSA has signed over 27 bilateral memorandums of understanding with various regulatory authorities around the world, including a unique mutual recognition model with Bank Negara of Malaysia to facilitate the cross-border flow of Islamic funds.

In the context of Islamic financial innovation, these actions are a step in the direction of streamlining and harmonizing the laws and regulations relating to Islamic finance. The ultimate objective should be an Islamic financial passport to facilitate cross-border trade in Islamic finance securities and the mutual recognition and establishment of Islamic financial institutions.

A strategic initiative of the government of Dubai was to establish the Dubai Multi Commodities Centre (DMCC) to create a level playing field for all participants in the gold and commodities industry by introducing transparent and fair rules for business conduct. The DMCC introduced an innovation, the Global Multi Commodities Receipt (GMR), as a tool to facilitate trade financing. Not limited to trade within the UAE, the GMR is composed of a Dubai Commodity Receipt (DCR: for Dubai-based deposits), the International Commodity Receipt (ICR: for selected international locations such as Singapore, Malaysia and South Korea) and the Dubai Gold Receipt (DGR: gold deposits in the UAE). The GMR is an electronic warehouse and vault receipt system that provides members with real-time access to the various forms of commodities, either raw, semi-finished or finished products stored in a DMCC-approved storage facility for that respective commodity.[5] GMRs are issued once a commodity deposit is recognized by an approved storage facility operator or collateral manager. Since GMRs are negotiable instruments, they are transferable to other traders or can be used as collateral to obtain financing. The GMR system provides Muslim and non-Muslim businesses with a secure electronic platform for interaction and conducting their trade finance activities.

Abu Dhabi

Compared with Dubai, Abu Dhabi has had significantly different challenges to become a financial centre in the region. While Dubai is strong on mergers and acquisitions, Abu Dhabi is strong on project finance, which has led the Royal Bank of Scotland to choose to centralize its

regional operations there after doing an extensive study of possible locations throughout the region.[6]

In 2005, the plan to launch the Ras Al Khaimah Financial City was also
approved. The idea is to develop an iconic financial city in the emirate.
The Ras Al Khaimah Financial City is the hub of the RAK Offshore project.
The expectation is that the city will become the new centre for financial
operations of the regional business community, offering financial, legal,
logistic and insurance services in a free zone environment. RAK Offshore
will be owned by Ras Al Khaimah Investment Authority and will facilitate
the operational and legislative requirements of the burgeoning emirate.[7]

Saudi Arabia

Traditionally a state that was much influenced by the west, Islamic finance
has made a comeback in Saudi Arabia for over the past decade. In May
2006, the Emaar Economic City (EEC) was incorporated by Dubai-based
Emaar Properties and a number of Saudi Arabian investors. It underwent
an initial public offering (IPO) in July 2006 to offer 30% of its shares on
the Saudi stock exchange (Tadawul). The main purpose of establishing the
EEC was to lead the development of the 168 million sq m King Abdullah
Economic City (KAEC) – the single largest private sector development in
the kingdom.

The KAEC, envisioned as a new age city being built today for tomorrow's
generation of Saudi citizens, started construction on December 21, 2005.
The aim is to integrate it into the kingdom's ongoing drive to expand the
economy, create employment opportunities for its young population and
function as a catalyst to attract foreign investment, global trade, commerce
and industry. The city's financial island was conceived to be a "city within
a city" for financial institutions, offering 500,000 sq m of office space for
the leading international and regional financial entities, business hotels
and a new exhibition and convention centre. It is estimated that 60,000
professionals are to operate daily from the financial island. The KAEC is
strategically located on the coast of the Red Sea between the two holy cities
of Mecca and Medina and the commercial hub of Jeddah. The project is
facilitated by the Saudi Arabian General Investment Authority.

Malaysia

In Malaysia, where 60% of the 27 million people are Muslim, government authorities have been promoting the area as a financial hub for Islamic finance. As part of the Central Bank of Malaysia's initiative to develop a range of financial instruments to manage short-term liquidity in the Malaysian Islamic interbank money market, the Commodity Murabaha House was established by Bank Negara Malaysia and the Malaysian Securities Commission, being a combination of eight Islamic banking institutions including three foreign-owned banking institutions. Employing the concept of *murabahah* and using crude palm oil as the underlying commodity, Bank Negara envisions the use of the instrument for liquidity management by financial institutions. The intention of this initiative is to provide an additional investment vehicle for Muslim investors in Southeast Asia and the Middle East who are looking to diversify their investment portfolios.

Dr Zeti Akhtar Aziz, Bank Negara Malaysia's governor, said the global financial crisis has thus far highlighted several structural weaknesses and imbalances in the international financial system: "Whilst Islamic finance is not insulated from the effects of the current environment, Shariah principles and the values that underlie Islamic finance provide an important underlying foundation."[8] Zeti claimed that Malaysia and London are well placed to become the new century's international finance hubs, with London leading western banking and Malaysia leading Islamic banking and finance. In her view, the integration of Islamic and western finance is essential, as the process of globalization has meant that Islamic finance has become increasingly exposed to the systemic implications of external developments.

Malaysia has been working hard to become the centre for Islamic asset management in the new century. Nevertheless, Malaysia is also strong in the area of *sukuk*, having the largest *sukuk* market at present. London currently has one of the most established exchanges. What the manager of Bank Negara suggests is that this is an area for potential cooperation, by cross-listing *sukuk*. Zeti said: "Putting in place a mechanism for sukuk issued in one jurisdiction to be recognised by the other would have a considerable impact on market accessibility, thereby allowing for greater issuer and investor reach."

Collaborating with the UK is also a logical step, claims the Malaysian bank manager, due to the UK's longstanding tradition of quality education. A joint programme between the University of Reading and the International Centre for Education in Islamic Finance in Malaysia is already underway.

The Malaysia International Islamic Financial Centre (MIFC), launched in 2006, continues the plan to promote Malaysia as a major hub for international Islamic finance. The MIFC is a collaborative effort by the country's financial and market regulators, including Bank Negara Malaysia, the Malaysian Securities Commission, Labuan Offshore Financial Services Authority and Bursa Malaysia (Kuala Lumpur's stock exchange). These work together with industry participation from the banking, *takaful* and capital market sectors in Malaysia. The objectives of the finance hub are to focus on the areas of *sukuk* origination, Islamic fund and wealth management, international Islamic banking, international *takaful* and human capital development.

Singapore

On January 19, 2009, the government of Singapore launched an S$200m (US$134m) Shariah-compliant sovereign *sukuk* designed specifically to attract foreign direct investment and to establish Singapore as an emerging regional centre for Islamic finance.[9] On a par with a Singapore Government Securities (SGS) and marketed with the nation's highest credit rating, "AAA", the Sukuk Al-Ijarah Trust Certificate Issuance Programme is issued by the Monetary Authority of Singapore.[10] Shariah scholars from the Islamic Bank of Asia and Standard Chartered Bank were the principle reviewers for compliance with Shariah principles. Singapore's strategy is threefold: to provide an investment vehicle for regional Muslims, to attract Middle Eastern petrodollars and to catch the attention of investors searching for ethical investing.

Hong Kong

A new area also striving to become an Islamic finance hub is the Chinese island enclave of Hong Kong, the world's third largest financial centre after New York and London. In March 2009, Hong Kong announced its budget, claiming that the Hong Kong Special Administrative Region government would send a draft law to the Legislative Council later in the year, aimed at creating a level playing field between Islamic financial products and conventional ones.[11]

The move has been widely welcomed by Islamic finance market players in the Asian region, the GCC countries and Europe. Hong Kong does not yet have an official Islamic financial strategy, but the new move to develop the island enclave into a regional and international Islamic capital markets hub is part of Hong Kong's strategy of being a global financial centre, offering opportunities in the fast-growing Islamic finance industry.

So far, several high-powered deals have come out of Hong Kong. Most of the HSBC *sukuk* mandates were structured by the bank's capital and debt market teams in Hong Kong, who worked closely with its dedicated Islamic finance division, HSBC Amanah. Explaining the government's Islamic finance strategy, Eddie Yue, the deputy chief executive of the Hong Kong Monetary Authority, stated:

> I believe that there is endless potential for us to innovate in the area of Islamic finance, especially in deploying our special strengths – our close affinity to China, our experience as an international fund raising centre and asset management hub, and our role as a testing ground for the Mainland's financial liberalization. There is no obstacle to Hong Kong becoming a centre for Islamic IPOs, given our distinct record as a leading IPO centre in the region. Now is the time to lay down the groundwork for future growth and development.[12]

Manama

In Manama, Bahrain, the Bahrain Financial Harbour (BFH), currently under construction, aims to serve the needs of individuals, groups and communities wanting to build business value and enhanced commercial success for their organizations. The BFH offers services including investment banks, commercial banks, offshore banking units, representative offices, *takaful* companies, legal and advisory services, fund managers, IT firms, professional institutes, *sukuk* and equity, leasing banks, international regulatory agencies, financial consultants and real estate investment trusts. At the 2007 Middle East Financial Services Summit, Stephen Rothel, CEO of Bahrain Finance House, said:

> This [the summit] has laid the ideal platform for the region to emerge as a leading global financial centre and Bahrain with its leadership position in both conventional and Islamic finance, along with its advanced regulatory framework, strategic position and robust multilateral trade agreements including WTO membership and an FTA agreement with the USA is well placed to take significant advantage of this. However, there are some limitations in terms of relatively less developed capital and bond markets and the lack of world-class technologically advanced infrastructure that is to some extent restricting this progress. BFH was conceived with the aim of addressing these concerns, in the

process significantly contributing to enhancing Bahrain and the region's position in the global financial markets.

Even more straightforwardly Shariah compliant than the BFH, the Bahrain Liquidity Management Centre (LMC) was established for the purpose of facilitating the investment of the surplus funds of Islamic banks and financial institutions into quality short- and medium-term financial instruments, structured in accordance with Shariah principles. The LMC offers a variety of *sukuk* products, fund structuring, issuance and documentation services.

Doha

In 2005, Qatar launched its own Finance Centre, in an attempt to rival both Bahrain and Dubai. It expects to appeal to commercial banking, project finance and asset managers as well as multinationals. Unlike the DIFC and Bahrain, Shariah-compliant banking and large back office operations are not a priority in the Qatar Finance Centre. The focus is more on boutique specialists servicing the local economy. The Barwa Financial District in Doha has also been seen as a giant project to serve the global, regional and local financial sector, but the Islamic finance component of the project is not as clear.

Mauritius

Situated between Africa, the Middle East, Southern Asia and Australia, the island nation of Mauritius is home to numerous domiciled conventional market investment funds. Favourable tax and economic treaties with over 40 nations provide a platform for Islamic finance with a unique value proposition – a centre of excellence to domicile Islamic investment funds similar to the conventional services they offer for fund administration. The Mauritian strategy is to act as a conduit for investment funds on a pan-regional scale, replicating services offered to conventional markets.

London

Outside the Muslim world, London has placed itself as the strongest Islamic finance centre. With all the strengths of a traditional financial centre, from a solid infrastructure to a qualified pool of prospective employees, London has managed to become a successful focal point for international Shariah-compliant investors, with both corporations and countries listing *sukuk* bonds in Britain. Taking advantage of New York's lack of interest in Islamic bonds or *takaful*, London continues to seek further influence on global Islamic finance. At present, the Islamic Bank of Britain, European Islamic Investment Bank, Europe Arab Bank, The Bank of London and The Middle East, Lloyds TSB and Barclays all provide Shariah-compliant products in the UK. There are also nine fund managers and a number of law firms specializing in Islamic finance. A vibrant secondary market exists for *sukuk*, which reached US$2bn a month in 2007.

France

A surprising new financial hub has emerged, as France has begun a process to encourage Islamic finance within its borders. After a pledge made in July 2008, the French government under President Sarkozy has brought in a series of detailed tax changes that will allow the rules of Islamic finance to be followed without attracting tax penalties, in comparison with other transactions. France is one of the world's leading economies, and attracts investment from around the world. The new government has endeavoured to make France a business-friendly environment, with the most favourable R&D tax credit in Europe. With over 6 million Muslims, three times the Muslim population of Britain, France is well placed to compete with the UK to become one of the most successful Islamic finance hubs outside the Muslim world.[13]

Australia

In Australia, Nail Aykan, senior manager, marketing and public relations, human resources of the Muslim Community Co-operative (Australia), claims that it is a matter of when, not if, a conventional bank sets up an Islamic window in Australia. He further identified two probable trends for the future of Islamic finance in Australia. The first suggests that there will be less focus on the absence of interest, as prohibition on interest is not the only feature of Islamic finance. Aykan claims that profit sharing, access to equity, and the idea of customers becoming partners with banks will be the principles to attract customers in Australia. It is also anticipated that there will be a lesser focus on Muslims in Australia, whereby the appeal of the products offered by the sector will broaden to people outside the minority Muslim community, as was the case in the UK.[14]

Specialization in a Globalized Economy

An analysis of the strategic plans proposed by each nation/city reveals an underlying theme, the desire to be a gateway to another region. Few proposals reveal the destination, only the potential of acting as a conduit to another capital market. What many national strategies fail to consider is that the term "gateway" is a misnomer, in that simply enabling access to excess financial capacity is only the beginning of a process, not the final result. Moreover, financial innovation in the macroeconomic sense centres on achieving a balance between the localization of products and the regionalization of regulatory structures. The attention has focused on creating greater diversity in product offerings needed to cater to local anomalies and cultural differences. However, achieving homogeneity in regulatory, legal and political agendas coupled with increasing degrees of standardization in Shariah interpretations presents multidisciplinary challenges.

Standardization or harmonization of Shariah-compliant financial products may be a practical impossibility because the nature of Islam is to be interpretive – adapting to the conditions and circumstances surrounding a transaction and striving to achieve equality between the parties sharing the risk and returns. The underlying opportunity is to increase communication between Shariah scholars, exposing them to the interpretations and decisions of other scholars, which in turn provides scholars with a wider knowledge base on which to base their interpretations. An increasing number of academics, regulators and industry analysts are calling for the expressed objective of Shariah standardization to increase the quality of financial activities. Although Shariah standardization or harmonization may be a noble objective, a more plausible goal is to increase the dialogue between scholars to cross-pollinate interpretations, bringing about Shariah synergies, which is an innovation in its own right. One such innovation could be the establishment of a central, national Shariah-compliant financial product database for Shariah scholars to enable them to share knowledge among colleagues and pass on interpretive logic to the next generation of Shariah scholars.

Specialization Does Not Mean Standardization

To harvest the unique set of economic, cultural and religious circumstances, regional Shariah-compliant financial services organizations must work in a strategic synergy with their governments to facilitate commerce. However, this type of macro-socioeconomic development strategy is predicated on banks and governments working together to take bold steps in the development of an interoperating financial infrastructure, taxation, and a fundamental rethinking of regulatory practices. The second generation of Islamic finance will see governments and financial institutions adopt collaborative mechanisms for meaningful exchange inside the region and, more importantly, with external entities.

Shariah-compliant banks of all sizes in emerging market economies face the same competitive challenges as their western counterparts, and perhaps many more, due to the frequency of political unrest, a lack of infrastructure, and socioeconomic imbalances. However, unlike western banks that strive for product/customer homogeneity, Islamic culture has adopted an approach of interpreting a set of fundamental beliefs that are adapted for the idiosyncrasies that have evolved over time in various geographic regions. The key differentiator between conventional banking practices that strive for sameness and Shariah-compliant financial practices that seek an equal exchange of value is the interpretive nature of how Shariah scholars account for cultural variations.

Islamic financial centres and individual institutions have the opportunity to develop specialized services that can be linked across institutions to form complementary financial product offerings. Among the challenges is the transformation of traditional individualized business relationships to an extra-regional network of Shariah-compliant financial services. Centres of financial competencies operating within each country linked by technology can act as linchpins to broker services throughout the Muslim world, connecting institutions within the region to each other and to external counterparts. This economic conduit takes the form of three unique value-added functions: a financial hub for capital mediation, an inter-regional business exchange, and a broker for aggregated goods and services to Muslim businesses.

Are Shariah-compliant Financial Institutions a Conduit for Global Business?

First, as a financial hub for capital mediation, for example, Shariah-compliant institutions operating in the Middle East and Malaysia can provide intermediary financial services connecting Eastern Europe, Africa and Southern Asia by mediating small/medium business capital markets into a virtual regional capital exchange. A virtual regional exchange linked with European, North American, Japanese and Australian markets provides a mechanism for infusions of global capital sources to regional businesses looking for financing and investments. Banks and other financial intermediaries offering Shariah-compliant services are in a unique position to lead a reinvention of financial services as they establish greater links between themselves, forming low-cost networks. These networks coupled with the rising demand for Islamic finance act as a precursor to economic development. Although collaboration between financial institutions is rare on this scale, the overwhelming need to increase capital flows throughout Muslim society creates a unique opportunity for banks, financial services institutions, government agencies and regulators to work together at an unprecedented level.

Second, as an inter-regional business and financial exchange, governments can develop incentives for companies to integrate the products and services found in the region with external consumer markets and, more importantly, global firms seeking new sources of goods and services. The microeconomic business climates found within emerging economies, many of which are home to Muslim societies, are predicated on a time-honoured tradition of building relationships between parties based on an implied trust and confidence that the expectations of delivery are met. This deep-seated attitude of trust and understanding between partners is the foundation for collaborative organization structure and the establishment of a competitive co-opetition marketplace, which operates by leveraging partnerships in a cooperative model.

Finally, as a broker for aggregated goods and services to regional businesses, exchange entities could bring together the requirements of small, medium and large businesses operating in the region and consolidate these into larger economic ordering quantities. This activity is vital for the region to maintain low-cost goods and services in a global economy. An aggregation exchange acts as a pathway for business to engage the services of a trading agent by which orders are consolidated, customs streamlined and international commerce becomes commonplace for any size of business operating in the region. In other words, these services make the services of international trade, typically reserved for big multinational businesses, accessible to every business in the region regardless of size or business volume. The necessary innovation is to develop a suite of financial services with sufficient product depth to accommodate local/regional capital needs, coupled with a significant increase in financial industry capacity.

The opportunities and challenges for Shariah-compliant financial institutions share a resemblance with the geographically distinct regions in Europe. Competition in these regional markets has to be addressed on three fronts:

- large global organizations expanding into the region

- new market entrants originating within the region

- new external entities brought into the region to establish operations with small local firms trying to grow market share.

Technology is the key to establishing a competitive differentiation that will continue to create an array of conditions to provide low-cost entry for new market entrants in many service sectors such as financial services, banking, commerce, energy and manufacturing.

In order to compete in the emerging global economy, Shariah-compliant financial institutions working with government agencies and regulators must create regional agendas to position cultural interests into a global perspective. Local interpretations of Shariah principles must factor in the importance of the issues of brand, technology proliferation, infrastructure, customer preference, social customs and religious variations. A simple framework can be employed to establish the relevance of a regional perspective:

- *think global* – combined commerce infrastructures

- *act regional* – product and services gateways

- *look local* – tailored service offerings.

Global Strategy

Global financial services companies have interpreted the globalization of banking services as standardization – providing a suite of generic products designed to reduce the overall cost of service delivery or processing. This homogeneous product philosophy is predicated on the concept that everyone in the world has similar banking needs, which revolve around a basic set of banking transactions: savings, payments and investments. Large institutions, such as HSBC Amanah, Barclays, Standard Chartered and others with significant conventional banking counterparts, have opted to use this operating philosophy to achieve economies of scale. This strategy enables a bank to focus on primary service delivery to the largest number of people with numerous delivery channels and branches. However, the vast majority of new market entrants into Islamic finance are relatively small and medium-sized organizations compared to their conventional counterparts, which limits the extent to which their operations can adopt this strategy. Newly formed organizations have identified market niches that centre on exploiting the differences in products, services and people. Niche market players clearly have a competitive advantage because of their ability to rapidly adapt to market conditions and develop offerings to service niche market opportunities.

The competitive advantage for small and medium-sized Shariah-compliant financial services companies is brand recognition and a greater propensity to provide a higher degree of customer service. Banks such as the UAE's Ajman Bank and Kenya's Gulf African Bank focus on specific market segments such as banking for women and specialized personal finance. The goal of a wider global reach by Shariah-compliant organizations is one dimension of market innovation, exemplified by Bahrain-based Al Baraka Banking Group's desire to create the world's biggest Islamic bank before the end of 2009, with an IPO of $3bn,[15] Kuwait Finance House's expansion into Saudi Arabia,[16] and Qatar Islamic Bank's expressed interest in expansion into the UK, Europe and the USA.

Regional Delivery

Contrary to the process of globalization is a movement towards the preservation of regional cultural values. There are many reasons for this phenomenon, but for our discussion on innovation, we would like to focus on two:

1 declining economic conditions are fostering a rise in nationalism

2 young Muslims are reaffirming their faith as they are exposed to western influences via television and the internet.

For Shariah-compliant banks, this re-engagement with cultural identity has a direct influence on the branding of Islamic finance in local markets, the structure of product offerings to reflect regional beliefs and provide a suite of services that incorporate the needs of many ethnic groups within the population. The opportunity for Shariah-compliant banks is to create regional business aggregation services that act to consolidate and broker primary business services to small and medium-sized enterprises (SMEs). Islamic banking institutions ultimately can provide basic outsourcing services such as payroll, cash management, investment management, accounts receivable and accounts payable. SME services are perhaps the most underserved segment within most emerging nations. Providing services to specific market segments and SMEs within local communities drives a number of strategic decisions by Islamic banks on the structure of their offerings, brand identity and levels of customer services. Smaller financial services providers can make a clear value choice on issues such as branding, driven by assessing the attitudes of the local customer base. In this sense, a Shariah-compliant institution may elect to retain its local branding and simply participate in the local business network.

Another innovation is collaboration among Shariah-compliant institutions on shared technological infrastructure. Banks are learning that customers do not care about, nor do they find any significant value in technological infrastructure, processing or any other back office activity. Islamic financial institutions have not advanced as far as their conventional counterparts along this line of thinking to develop shared infrastructure or the provision of white-labelled services. The opportunity for innovation across the emerging markets for Shariah-compliant banks is to cooperate in the use of technological infrastructure such as card processing, payment switches and credit assessment services. Collaborative Shariah-compliant financial networks enable institutions to alter their product offerings and brand identities, such as co-branding with a larger institution for a wider market appeal and/or brokering services via the aggregated marketplace. Consequently, an Islamic bank may choose to co-brand in a particular geography and remain locally branded in others, while utilizing a shared regional infrastructure.

Localization and Specialization of Products

The vast majority of Muslims worldwide conduct their business activities without the support of a Shariah-compliant financial infrastructure or access to capital from Islamic financial sources. Consequently, most commerce that is originated by Muslims, or where Muslims are the recipient of commercial transactions, is conducted in conventional financial markets or within mixed economies. Thus there are numerous market opportunities for Islamic financial institutions in emerging nations to provide commercial banking services. Equally, there is a reciprocal opportunity for Shariah-compliant financial institutions to provide retail banking and consumer financing. During the past 10 years, Islamic financial institutions have learned that, in national economies where there is little or no Shariah-compliant banking, simply providing basic banking services is enough to gain market share and establish operations. However, as more institutions enter local markets, the nature of competition changes, forcing a bank to offer a more sophisticated product suite to attract and retain customers. Thus, localization of Shariah-compliant financial products will be an area requiring much needed innovation.

The Opportunity for Specialization and Co-opetition

Shared services, collaborative technological infrastructure, consumer behaviour, defined market segments and other cultural factors have created the conditions for co-opetition between Shariah-compliant financial services providers in many emerging nations. Technology is presenting the banks operating in these regions with an opportunity to leverage the resources of the region to compete with their Western counterparts on a level playing field. One role of national governments is to develop the necessary regulatory environment for cooperative commerce to flourish. More importantly, governments must strive to create the market conditions and social infrastructures for Shariah-compliant banks to grow and become viable corporate entities in the long term. Therefore, Shariah-compliant institutions can only grow at a defined rate, which is limited by their access to investment capital under existing market conditions. Governments have an unprecedented opportunity to facilitate global commerce and be the originator of a new era in global economic collaboration by developing cohesive agendas in which regulatory adaptations can promote Islamic finance at an accelerated rate.

In the context of innovation in Islamic financial markets, market growth is proportional to two key factors:

1 government policy support in the form of banking reform, regulatory changes and monetary policy synchronization

2 an individual financial institution's appetite for risk as a product of innovation.

The first factor – governments creating an economic environment where banks can reduce their costs by collaborating and capitalizing on other market opportunities – is, for the most part, beyond the control of most

Islamic banks' management teams. The second factor – balancing the risk/ innovation equation – is squarely within the power of most senior managers to make demonstrable changes within the organization. Perhaps the most immediate opportunity for Shariah-compliant banks is to serve the vast number of unbanked people in Muslim and non-Muslim nations.

Dr Zeti Akhtar Aziz, governor of Malaysia's central bank, notes that in the context of the Islamic finance industry: "Innovation is key to sustaining growth and securing competitive advantage."[17] According to Aziz, the potential value of Islamic finance can only be realized through a process of innovating new Islamic financial products and services to increase the range in order to fulfil the sophisticated and complex requirements of today's consumers and businesses. The introduction of a vast array of new products demands greater efficiency in the development of products, distribution of banking services and higher levels of customer services. As Shariah-compliant financial institutions strive for greater efficiencies and new products, the institutions themselves will undergo a transition. As financial service providers try to maintain an agenda of growth, they will turn their attention towards channel innovation by expanding into new markets. To expand into new markets, launch new products and leverage their service delivery capabilities, Shariah-compliant financial institutions are using technology as a basis for innovation. Islamic financial institutions are employing technology in two distinct ways: to offer more products and to reach more people.

Notes

1 Dubai Islamic Bank outlines 2009 growth strategy, Dubai Islamic Bank, press release, March 9, 2009.

2 Gulf Africa Bank statistics from interview with author, Nairobi, February 18, 2009.

3 D.C. Johnson, CEO and chief investment strategist, Calyx Financial, interview with the authors, October, 2008.

4 Dubai International Finance Centre, www.difc.ae/.

5 The first online electronic warehouse receipt platform in the region with global coverage, Dubai Multi Commodities Centre, www.dmcc.ae.

6 Will Abu Dhabi become a global financial centre?, AMEInfo, November 21, 2007, www.ameinfo.com/139312.html.

7 Rakeen announces the development of Ras Al Khaimah, June 12, 2007, www.raktourism.com/ListNews.aspx?id=31.

8 Malaysia, London can bridge Islamic financial markets, 25/2/2009, www.mysinchew.com/node/21669.

9 Singapore plans S$200 million Islamic bond programme, Reuters, January 19, 2009, www.reuters.com/article/rbssBanks/idUSSGC00098220090119.

10 Islamic Bank of Asia in Singapore *sukuk* job, CPI Financial, January 20, 2009, www.cpifinancial.net.

11 Hong Kong eyes Islamic finance, Arab News, February 23, 2009, www.arabnews.com/?p age=6&section=0&article=119493&d=23&m=2&y=2009.

12 Hong Kong eyes Islamic finance, Arab News, February 23, 2009, www.arabnews.com/?p age=6&section=0&article=119493&d=23&m=2&y=2009.

13 France on track to be one of world's centres for Islamic finance, Islamic Finance Advisory & Assurance Services, press release, April 3, 2009.

14 N. Aykan, senior manager, marketing and public relations, human resources, Muslim Community Co-operative Australia, interview with the authors, October, 2008.

15 Morris, M., Islamic mega bank on course for launch, March 31, 2009, www.arabianbusiness.com/.

16 KFH plans $133.3 million Saudi investment branch, Arab Times, April 4, 2009, www.arabtimesonline.com/kuwaitnews/pagesdetails.asp?nid=30772&ccid=12.

17 Islamic finance: promoting the competitive advantage, keynote address by Dr Zeti Akhtar Aziz, governor of Bank Negara Malaysia, at the Islamic Bankers' Forum 2005, Islamic Finance: Promoting Competitive Advantage, Putrajaya, June 21, 2005.

4

NEW FORMS OF CAPITAL FOR TWENTY-FIRST-CENTURY BUSINESS

As conventional capital markets continue to operate under stressed conditions in 2009, the central debate among industry analysts, academics, practioners and governments is whether or not Islamic finance can provide an answer to the challenges inherited from free-market capitalism. Supporters of Islamic finance enthusiastically pronounce a Shariah-compliant banking model as a cure-all for the current credit crisis and global economic woes, while detractors claim that it merely disguises the charging of interest through clever financial engineering.

Macroeconomists rightly point out that although there is an underlying sense of fair play and self-regulation behind Islamic finance, the system has never been subject to large-scale transaction volumes or suffered any substantial asymmetric economic shocks. Similarly, market critics note that a large portion of the industry's growth is happening in tax-free environments. This raises the question: is Islamic finance destined to take over from free-market capitalism? That question would, however, require several books in their own right. For our discussion, we will examine the question of Islamic finance as a viable, sustainable model for transnational business as it relates to Islamic financial innovation.

Several key factors should be addressed in the context of Islamic financial innovation on an industry-wide global scale:

- the lack of data with which to model the economic activities and impact of Islamic finance on a transnational basis

- the rising problems of liquidity for Shariah-compliant institutions

- the formation of stronger trading agreements between emerging nations

- the formation of monetary/currency unions.

As research continues to help us to understand the interplay of Islamic finance within the communities served by the current and emerging products, one thing become clear, Islamic finance plays a significantly different role in facilitating the economy of a nation. Shariah-compliant institutions are investment-oriented financial intermediaries acting somewhat in the same way as government economic development agencies, and as a result, their activities often lead to the sustainability of the socioeconomic order and the perpetuation of community assets. Historically, the co-dependent relationship between a financial institution and the community has not been confined to Shariah-compliant institutions or indeed to Islamic finance, as this relationship between bank and community has been well known in Christian societies during the past six centuries. For example, the Monte dei Paschi Bank, founded in 1472 by the Free Republic of Siena, Italy, was initially considered a state institution and its activities were strictly regulated.[1] The Monte dei Paschi Bank is home to one of the first known examples of a printed letter of credit (c. 1646), a financial mechanism learned from Arab traders.

Theoretically, the role of a Shariah-compliant institution is to provide access to capital as an equitable financial intermediary. During the first generation of Islamic finance development, most activities concentrated on large financial deals between big businesses or real estate development. Access to financial deals was often limited to the parties brokering the deals, with little or no opportunity for small investors to participate. Financial deals are traditionally based on a model of an equitable partnership or joint venture-like structure that to some extent has limited participation. This raises an important point when considering the spread of Islamic financial innovation to non-Muslim-dominated nation states, as partnerships are the least favoured form of business association in western societies. This has been noted by Farooq:

> An important constraint ignored by the Islamic discourse is that partnership is the least common type of business organization, due to certain inherent problems associated with partnership. Those problems are real, and human behaviour in such business organizational contexts is not irrational in avoiding the kind of PLS [profit/loss sharing] and risk-sharing modes.[2]

In Farooq's view, the parameters for profit/loss sharing under classical

Islamic law limit the extent to which today's Shariah-compliant banks can structure their products. Consequently, innovation must come more from the interpretation of Shariah principles by contemporary scholars and less on traditional Islamic legal discourse. This is not to imply that Islamic finance will reject in any way the traditional legal interpretations of Shariah law. It does imply that contemporary Islamic scholars will place issues of Shariah-compliant banking products into a modern context to provide Muslims in the twenty-first century with banking products that best facilitate their lifestyles. This does not imply a relaxation of Shariah compliance, rather, it indicates that no single interpretation that can be applied globally. The interpretive nature of Shariah principles is the strength of Islamic finance to best fit the needs of Muslims.

The Historical Role of Islamic Financial Innovation on Macroeconomics

Although most Americans and Europeans would like to believe that innovation in financial services emanates from US or European financial centres, the Middle East and Southeast Asia have a historical legacy of financial innovations. In the ninth century, for example, a Muslim trader could cash a cheque in China drawn on his bank in Baghdad.[3] The modern word "cheque" comes from the Arabic *sakk* – a written promise to pay for goods when they were delivered, to avoid money having to be transported across dangerous terrain.[4] Put simply, a cheque is a bill of exchange drawn on a bank and payable on demand.[5] Historically, necessity has been the mother of invention in Islamic finance, which is consistent with the interpretive nature of Shariah law. Innovations such as the cheque or bills of exchange were created out of the necessity of the operating environment in which trade occurred at that time. Bills of exchange migrated to Europe, and become a financial tool for medieval Italian bankers. The popular modern view is that medieval bills of exchange were to thwart bandits during travel – the creation of these banking mechanisms was to reduce losses and facilitate a more convenient form of transaction. This overlooks two other facets of bills of exchange at that time: they provided a practical mechanism for international credit and currency exchange, and they avoided usury (forbidden by the Christian Church).[6] The process of early implementation and subsequent maturity of bills of exchange is similar to the innovation and technical evolution happening in contemporary Shariah-based financial services. Throughout history, therefore, Islamic finance has followed a clear path of adaptation in its practices, which has facilitated its viability into the present day.

In the early years of the twenty-first century, we find three major economic systems: capitalist, socialist and Islamic. Capitalism and socialism have coexisted and interacted with enormous transactions for many decades, while the Islamic economic system remained relatively small in comparison. During the 2000s, the Islamic economic system has emerged as a viable alternative market for business, commerce and the facilitation of consumer banking. Growing in volume and maturing in regulatory structures, the Islamic economic system is engaging academics, economists and governments in debate as to how to strengthen governmental oversight and industry self-regulation to avoid the asymmetric shocks suffered by the economies based on capitalist and socialist values.

It is well known that the capitalist system rests on the belief that wealth should be distributed among those who have taken a part in producing it (known as the "factors of production"). The four factors of production are:

- *capital* – cash or commodity used to generate income

- *labour* – active work

- *land* – natural resources, as yet untouched by human production

- *organization* – the factor that brings together the first three by applying labour and bearing the risk and loss in the production.

The wealth produced is meant to be distributed in four, not necessarily equal shares (one to capital, as interest; one to labour, as wages; one to land, as rent; and one to the organization, as profit).[7] Unlike the capitalist system, under the socialist economy, capital and land are not private, but belong to the community, and the organization is the state itself. Profit and interest therefore disappear, at least in theory, from the socialist economy.[8]

The Islamic system has a different view of the distribution of wealth to that of the capitalist and the socialist systems. According to Usmani, in the Islamic view, there are two groups entitled to wealth – those who participate directly in the process of production, and those who have a secondary right, as they did not directly participate in the process of production, but have enjoined the producers to make them co-sharers in their wealth. As in the capitalist system, those who have a primary right to wealth form part of one of the four factors, except that in the Islamic system, there are only three factors: capital, assets (land and machines that can be leased) and labour. The shares of wealth are divided, not necessarily equally, into three parts (capital receives its share in the form of profit, rather than interest; land receives its share as rent; and labour receives its share as wages).[9]

The Islamic economic system differs fundamentally from the socialist economic system in that it accepts private property, which does not exist in the socialist system. The Islamic system views private property as economically natural, and the socialist economy's rejection of that principle suggests that, from an Islamic economic perspective, socialism denatures the economic order.[10] The Islamic economy compares to the capitalist system by rewarding capital with profit, rather than interest. Capital is also defined more generically than in the capitalist system, and includes machinery and any necessary foodstuff. Land is also defined more comprehensively as anything that is not wholly consumed to be used in the production. Likewise, labour incorporates mental work and planning in its definition.[11] The ability to take risks belongs to the capital itself, which is different from what is understood by the capitalist system.

A New Dawn

The significant difference between these three economic ideologies is the level at which government agencies, businesses, financial institutions and international agencies interact to facilitate the new industry. Another aspect of government intervention is the degree of involvement by government agencies in the transnational promotion of Islamic finance, irrespective of existing international treaties, or lack of international treaties. As an industry, the future of Islamic finance is more than simply inventing new products or applying new technologies. The future is about providing access to financial services that are Shariah compliant. In many cases, the primary reason governments are evaluating Islamic finance and taking measures to accommodate its introduction into their countries is not that the products are better, cheaper or ethically constructed, rather, it is because the vast majority of the population in most countries has no access to any financial services. So, lacking a financial infrastructure, any movement towards providing any services that will engage the public and bring capital into the formal economy is most welcome. From an economic perspective, Muslims will have more financial options, additional places and ways to use financial services that comply with their fundamental beliefs, while indirectly participating in the economic development of their country. Furthermore, because of the investments being made by Shariah-compliant institutions, more people (Muslims and non-Muslims) will have access to banking services. In many emerging economies, Islamic financial institutions are leading the way to provide services to underbanked populations previously ignored by conventional banks. To Muslim businesses (and non-Muslim businesses), Islamic financing is a viable alternative for their financial needs. This understanding is becoming clear as western economies and their associated capital markets continue to experience a great deal of volatility.

Economic Unions and the Role of the US Dollar

We must reconsider the definition of the US dollar as the world's de facto currency in our discussion on the global phenomena that are changing how innovation is being applied in Islamic finance. Clearly, as US economic conditions deteriorate and nations shift increasing percentages of their currency reserves out of US dollars, there are direct and indirect implications for Islamic finance. The global financial crisis is acting as a catalyst to redefine financial markets in favour of Islamic finance. Action such as the establishment of a regional monetary union and a single currency assist the regional financial sector by providing adequate market infrastructure for Islamic finance to move into a third generation of financial innovation. To achieve greater market penetration and better facilitate economic activities within nations and transnational commerce, Islamic finance must have a higher degree of liquidity. For example, Shariah-compliant debt instruments such as *sukuk* suffer from a lack of short-term conversion as they tend to carry long maturities. This prevents the development and growth of a secondary market because investors are looking for maturities of three, four or six months, which are significantly shorter periods.[12] At the same time, in 2008, the US dollar lost its place as the currency of choice for *sukuk*, with only about 10% of issues raised in this currency.[13]

Managing Risk

First, the various lending structures generate different risks and balance sheet exposures for Islamic banks that need to be carefully monitored and managed. For example, as Taylor argued, while only a few Islamic financial products generate different liquidity profiles from conventional products, it is the lack of uniformity in Islamic banking practices that makes it difficult to apply the same prudent regulatory standards across the board.[14] This calls for the further harmonization of Islamic banking practices as well as Shariah standards. Unless these two elements are synchronized at the national and international levels, Islamic finance may be seen as more risky than traditional forms of finance.

Islamic financial innovation is the new paradigm, which acts to combine the financing of business activities, national economic development, and the financial requirements of individual communities and Muslim society. In the design of new products, Islamic financial institutions must concentrate their efforts on aligning their operations, strategic plans, systems and products to ensure the profitability of the institution and to act as a facilitator of socioeconomic development. This presents a challenge to the management team of a Shariah-compliant institution as profits are easily measured and understood by shareholders, while the impact on the overall development of society is much harder to quantify. Therefore, management teams must develop concise measures to combine the goals of economic efficiency (growth) of the institution and social justice through various outlets of corporate social responsibility. Management teams must show a causal relationship between actions they perform. For example, financing affordable housing, which can be demonstrated by an increase in the number of people in the lower third of the economic pyramid within a community living in new homes. A model of socioeconomic development based on complementary goals between the financial institution and the community it serves is substantially different from the relationship between banks and consumers in conventional financial markets.

Innovations in three directions are crucial: liquidity enhancement, risk transfer and revenue generation. In its early days, Islamic finance had to focus on revenue generation as it had to compete with conventional finance and show comparable returns. Times have changed. The need to enhance liquidity, and hence to move towards greater securitization of assets, is already recognized, as shown by the developments in Malaysia. The bottleneck at the present seems to be risk management.

An Interest-free Economy?

In the current economic climate, economists, academics, politicians, regulators and the media are engaged in a great debate on the causes of the economic decline under the western capitalist model. Advocates of Islamic finance have trumpeted the attributes of interest free, fair play and equality, founded in a set of moral constructs, as the answer to the economic problems of the day. However, from the perspective of Islamic innovation, it is prudent to review briefly a few principles at the heart of the economic discourse: money, time and the generation of value. These concepts are important to Islamic innovation because they offer the basis on which innovation must generate new products, while limiting what is possible under the governing moral standard.

Over the past four decades, economists have developed economic models of increasing complexity and sophistication to explain the expansion and contraction of international economic output, the rise and fall of interest rates and corporate share prices. With each generation of economic analysis, the quantity of numeric variables increases, the relationship of numbers to other numbers is redefined and the total depth of quantitative analysis grows in tandem with the capabilities offered by each successive generation of computer equipment. Ironically, as economists generate ever increasing volumes of data on economic trends and their meaning, we are just as exposed to economic bubbles and declines as previous generations of bankers. Often overlooked, or ignored because of their complexity, are the basic principles of human nature: fear of the future, individualistic greed, and either a sense of obligation that binds people within society together or the sense of preservation, which sets people apart.[15] Often we overlook the fact that a financial system is simply a collection of contractual obligations, whose nature and characteristics, maintained within a legal framework, define the system.[16] Contracts are at the heart of the discussion on what comprises the foundation of a non-interest-based financial system. Fundamentally, the prime differentiator between contractual obligations is the fixed return of the principal amount lent versus the sharing of the returns from productive outputs made from loaned money.

One question arises as Islamic finance continues to mature: does Islamic finance open a door to an alternative economic system? This question has been discussed in academic circles over the past decade and with renewed interest since 2008. The root of this debate centres historically on the inequalities of liberal capitalism, specifically on the role interest plays in striking a balance between the social classes. At different times in history, economists, such as Silvio Gesell, Irwin Fisher and John Maynard Keynes, who expressed concern regarding the social pressures and strains that interest creates, have explored the possibility of an interest-free monetary system.[17]

In 1906, Silvio Gesell, a German merchant who moved to Buenos Aries during the height of the Argentine depression, wrote *The Natural Economic Order*, a reflection of the structural problems caused by the monetary system. In the 1930s, John Maynard Keynes reviewed Gesell's work, commenting on Gesell's theory describing interest as belonging to the quality of money, being purely a monetary occurrence setting a limit on the growth rate of real capital. In Keynes' view, a non-interest-based economic system warranted closer examination and was conceivably viable. Gessell's evaluation of zero-interest economies advocated that money should be used to stimulate consumption rather than to earn interest. If one looks at the fundamental tenets of the Islamic value proposition, the potential reduction of money circulating in the economy does not determine zero interest.[18] Rather, the Islamic theory of zero interest is based on the idea that the time value of money (profit) is acceptable, but the monetary value of time (interest) is not.

In 1958, Islamic economist Mahmout Abu Saud also wrote about Gesell's free money theory:

> Gesell's theory of interest is in harmony with the teaching of the Koran and should be welcomed in all Islamic countries. His plan for an interest-free economy is a solid basis for constructive attempts to liberate man from the slavery of his own illusions, from the tyranny of mistaken tradition, and from exploitation by his fellowman.[19]

Perhaps with the further development of Gesell's ideas, Islamic banking will be at a crucial position to help to develop an alternative economic system, one fundamentally different from the liberal capitalism that we now know.

Gesell's Interest-free Theory

John Maynard Keynes, who noted that Gesell's concept of a fair and equitable economy needed more study, gave us a clue as to why the world is now looking at Islamic finance with new eye: "Capitalism is the astounding belief that the most wickedest of men will do the most wickedest of things for the greatest good of everyone." Advocates of an interest-free monetary system often advocate the use of gold or silver as the basis for establishing the value of money. Although money systems were traditionally founded on the use of these metals, they fail to meet the needs of modern Muslim society such as ease of transportation, storage and use. However, these commodities are also subject to inflation and the added costs of handling, which make them unable to facilitate all the needs of commerce in an integrated economic system. Gesell's concept of interest-free money suggests that money must originate from and be controlled by a central authority (central bank) to ensure that it cannot be created independently by banks themselves. In Gesell's view, the introduction of a user fee on money overcomes the negative consequences of interest. In addition, private ownership of money is prohibited as money is a public institution (money must continually move and not be hoarded). However, private ownership of money credits in the form of claims on money such as savings and securities replicates key financial instruments.

So how does Gesell's monetary system work without interest (free money) as a basis of return on investment? Theoretically, there is a direct relationship between the circulation of money and economic boom and bust cycles. When money is created, it must circulate on a regular basis to facilitate commerce and act as an engine of economic growth. In conventional monetary systems, the circulation of money is a product of two key functions of money: trading and borrowing. People are motivated to trade money in the form of purchasing goods or services, which is motivated by the necessity of satisfying human needs. The second form of circulation is through borrowing, which is motivated by interest. Interest is the "price" of using money, and ensures that unspent money is lent to other people. In this way, money is not hoarded by people, which means it circulates freely.

Sceptics claim that a monetary system based on a currency of declining value cannot work, yet historically there is evidence to the contrary. The Austrian town of Wörgl conducted a successful experiment, known now as the "economic miracle of Wörgl", which was eventually shut down by national regulators because it threatened to unseat the autonomy of the incumbent monetary system, and was brought to the attention of the French parliament by French President Daladier.[20]

By 1932, Wörgl had a population of 4,300 people, a 35% unemployment rate, factories had closed, taxes were in arrears and the town was no longer economically viable. These conditions provided the foundation for a bold experiment to establish an interest-free economic system based on Gesell's natural economic order. To change the social dynamics and economic climate, a local relief committee was formed to produce jobs by creating an alternative currency designed to circulate without interest. Placing 5,490 Austrian shillings into reserve to act as a guarantee fund, the town issued 5,490 "work certificates".[21] This money was designed to lose value at a rate of 1% per month. To maintain full face value, the holder of the money had to purchase a stamp worth 1% that represented a usage fee. As Kennedy notes:

The fee acts as a "circulation incentive" limiting money to its function as a means of exchange and as a stable means for storing value. If you have more money than you need, you take it to the bank, which lends it out, returning it to circulation, and then there is no fee.[22]

According to Fisher, the results were clearly measurable:

> the currency circulated 463 times in 13.5 months, creating goods and services worth 5,490 x 463 or over 2,283,840 million schillings. At a time when most countries in Europe had a decreasing number of jobs, Wörgl reduced its unemployment rate by 25 percent within a year. Income from local taxes rose 35 percent and investment in public works 220 percent. The fee collected by the town government which caused the money to change hands so quickly amounted to 12 percent of 5,490 Schillings or a total of 658 Schillings.[23]

Although at first the concept of interest-free money seems confusing or at best unsettling when contrasted with currency systems, little would change from the perspective of customers. Money in a cheque account would be treated like cash and subject to the circulation fee, while money in a savings account would be free of the fee, retaining its value and so preserving an incentive to save. A borrower would have to pay for the bank's services in addition to a risk premium, both fees that are currently included as a small part of each loan.

The absence of a predetermined interest rate would lead to a financial system based on equity and with less interference from central authority, which usually uses the interest rate to control the economy. In a Shariah-based system, the rate of returns of financial assets is measured by and against a benchmark of a real rate of returns of a similar investment of that sector of investment and economy.

Innovative ideas such as Gesell's free money could meet many of the requirements of a Shariah-compliant monetary system. As the industry continues to mature, the need to address the fundamental structures of monetary systems will undoubtedly rise to the top of the debate on innovations needed within Islamic finance.

Topology of the Islamic Finance Industry

Since the late 1990s, as an industry, Islamic finance has undergone a significant transformation from small banks operating within two regional markets to becoming a key participant in the global marketplace. In a historical context, Islamic finance is now entering its renaissance period – adapting and changing to meet the needs of modern finance – which has gained the attention of large global financial institutions. At the end of 2008, the Islamic finance industry represented US$639bn in assets accompanied by a 27% year-on-year growth rate. However, when compared with around US$70 trillion of conventional banking assets worldwide, Islamic finance accounts for only a small fraction of the global banking marketplace. However, within the context of the global market, Islamic finance is the only sector of the market that has shown consistent growth during the past five years, while conventional markets during the same period have declined. Thus, the value of the Islamic financial marketplace is estimated to reach US$1trillion by 2010. When these market statistics are coupled with the fact that less than 8% of the global 1.6 billion Muslims use banking of any kind, we can see that there are enormous opportunities for innovation in products, services and distribution in this market.

As of December 2008, the Islamic finance industry comprised approximately 1,030 institutions advertising some form of Shariah-compliant financial service. The market comprises three types of institutions: large conventional banks operating an Islamic window, regional Islamic financial institutions, and small local banks. The market is dominated by 20 larger institutions (61.5% of the total market), 30 medium-sized institutions (19.5% of total market) and 980 smaller institutions. Therefore, the top 50 banks represent 81% of the total assets of the Shariah-compliant industry.

Enticed by the potential of this market, global banks have set up operations in many countries throughout the region. As the market for Shariah-compliant banking grows, matures and evolves, one thing is evident: in order to compete, local banks will have to make some difficult strategic decisions. Should a bank compete on product innovation, fee structure, quality of service or operationally excellent cost structure? A bank's strategy will determine its ultimate success or failure, because if market conditions continue, inevitably the market for financial services providers will have to consolidate.

An examination of the top 20 Islamic financial institutions reveals two types of Shariah-based organizations: those where 100% of their operations are Shariah compliant and those that have implemented Shariah-compliant banking windows (Table 4.1). Iranian banks dominate the market as far as assets are concerned, while banks in other parts of the Middle East dominate the vast majority of customers and the bulk of the transaction volume. Kuwait Finance House and Dubai Islamic Bank are market leaders, which is reflected in their growing product portfolios, with HSBC Amanah adding a global reach to Shariah-compliant banking. The relative size of these organizations, illustrated in Figure 4.1, indicates that the size of the organization is not a determining factor in the organization's ability to innovate. In the case of the top 18 largest Shariah-compliant institutions, innovation (and the spending associated with innovation) is primarily a product of the ambitions of senior management and the willingness of the Shariah boards to tolerate a process of trial and error.

Table 4.1 Top 20 Islamic Financial Institutions, 2008					
	Institutions	Type	Assets	% Change	Country
1	Bank Melli Iran, Tehran	S	48,469.87	20.97	Iran
2	Al Rajhi Bank	S	33,347.53	18.70	Saudi Arabia
3	Bank Saderat Iran, Tehran	S	32,610.00	16.94	Iran
4	Bank Mellat, Tehran	S	32,533.60	25.62	Iran
5	Kuwait Finance House	S	31,861.73	39.34	Kuwait
6	Bank Tejarat, Tehran	S	26,340.00	17.12	Iran
7	Bank Sepah, Tehran	S	24,142.40	39.88	Iran
8	Dubai Islamic Bank	S	22,801.57	29.96	UAE
9	Bank Keshavarzi, Tehran	S	16,298.00	24.13	Iran
10	HSBC Amanah	S	15,194.00	56.24	UK
11	Parisian Bank	S	15,117.36	44.21	Iran
12	Bank Maskan Iran, Tehran	S	13,075.00	n/a	Iran
13	Abu Dhabi Islamic Bank	S	12,063.39	22.08	UAE
14	Al Baraka Banking Group	S	11,167.47	29.25	Bahrain
15	Bank Rakyat	S	10,397.07	26.95	Malaysia
16	National Commercial Bank Ltd, Jeddah	W	10,358.34	12.89	Saudi Arabia
17	Riyad Bank	W	9,932.18	32.89	Saudi Arabia
18	Maybank Islamic	S	7,755.05	n/a	Malaysia
19	Saudi British Bank (SAAB)	W	7,351.13	27.77	Saudi Arabia
20	Samba Financial Group	W	6,885.45	16.52	Saudi Arabia
Source: Maris Strategies and *The Banker*, November 2008					
Key: S = Shariah-compliant institutions, W = conventional bank with Shariah window					

Economic conditions during the next 10 years may align to consolidate the Islamic finance market on a local/regional scale. There are a number of possible outcomes, as smaller institutions either close or merge with each

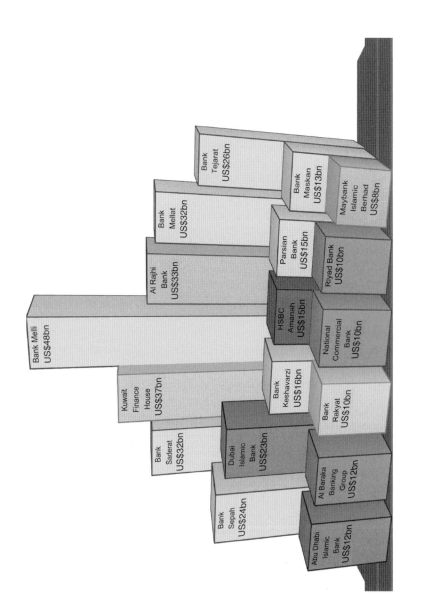

Figure 4.1 Relative Size of the 18 Largest Shariah-compliant Institutions

other to create a number of medium-sized banks, or smaller banks may be bought by larger banks to increase their geographic distribution network or to acquire an existing customer base. An example of this is the merger of Emirates Bank International and the National Bank of Dubai, which has created a larger regional bank, Emirates NBD.

Islamic financial institutions are still growing. The global economic crisis has reduced or delayed most banks' expansion plans, but for the most part, Islamic financial institutions are still growing. During 2007 to 2009, HSBC Amanah, for example, grew by 56%, Dubai Islamic Bank grew by 30%, Kuwait Finance House by 28%, Al Rajhi Bank by 18% and Pasargard Bank in Iran grew by a staggering 158% during the same period. Growth is coming from three different directions:

1 *Existing customers:* they are putting more money into banks. One reason for this might relate to the US Patriot Act 2001, which declares that any transaction coming in or out of America greater than US$5,000 has to be scrutinized by the government, so funds traditionally invested in Wall Street are now remaining in home markets. Thus, investment growth in the Middle East is partly fuelled by money that used to go abroad.

2 *New customers:* the vast majority of populations in the Middle East, Africa and Southeast Asia are underbanked, so a sizable amount of growth is the result of providing access to financial services in communities that have been excluded from financial services under conventional banking regimes.

3 *Expanding markets into new territories:* moving into previously unbanked populations or nations that have significant Muslim populations with little or no access to Shariah-compliant services provides these customers with new services.

Contrasting the number of Shariah-compliant banks and their product offerings (depth of financial services) against the total Muslim population by nation gives an approximate relative size of each national market, as shown in Figure 4.2. The analysis of the size and depth of Shariah-compliant banking services provided in each country relative to the markets they serve indicates a clear mismatch of the capacity of the Islamic finance market. For example, the most populous Muslim nations such as Indonesia, Pakistan and Bangladesh have the least or at best a marginal access to Shariah-compliant services. Nations in the Gulf Cooperation Council (GCC) with relatively small Muslim populations have the

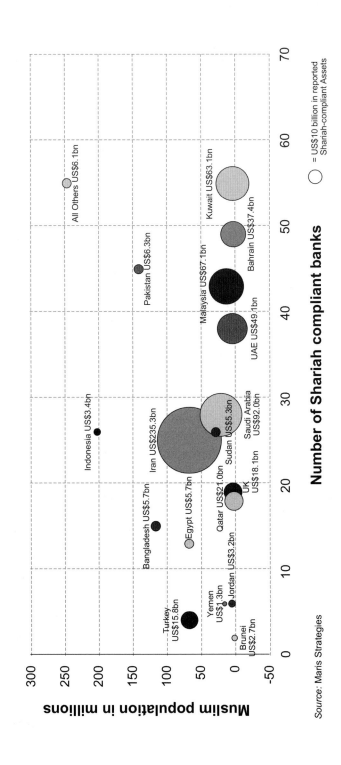

Figure 4.2 Shariah-compliant Bank Density by Country

Source: Maris Strategies

greatest access to Shariah-compliant services. Within the GCC, the populations and associated Shariah-compliant banking services are concentrated within urban areas, thus the depth of service is limited to the availability of technological infrastructure. Figure 4.2 shows that an opportunity exists for Islamic banks to migrate to nations with larger Muslim populations.

A examination of the category "all others" in Figure 4.2 reveals that approximately 245 million Muslims living in 17 countries have access to around 55 Shariah-compliant finance institutions (see Figure 4.3).

An analysis of the nations depicted in Figure 4.3 reveals two key features of Islamic finance globally: a highly fragmented marketplace and a significant potential for growth. The market for Shariah-compliant financial services is composed of emerging customer segments, which have their own distinct cultural needs, requirements for facilitating customer lifestyles and preferences for financial instruments. In some markets where the Muslim population has had adequate access to conventional financial services, the preferences for financial instruments have been shaped by the features and functions of conventional banking and investment products. Financial institutions operating in these markets are developing strategies that include product innovation and channel delivery innovation.

In markets where populations have had little or no access to financial services, the level of customer sophistication is less developed, creating additional challenges for Islamic institutions. Shariah-compliant institutions in less developed markets must also develop a strategy that includes innovation in three distinct areas: product, distribution and customer education. Market fragmentation in many of these emerging markets reduces the overall effectiveness of mass marketing techniques and erodes brand loyalty. The level of fragmentation in the Islamic finance marketplace at this stage of its development is expected. As the distribution of Shariah-compliant banking services becomes more widespread across global populations, market conditions will present an opportunity whereby consolidation of the market becomes a plausible eventuality to improve cost efficiencies within institutions striving to achieve economies of scale. Reducing the cost of distribution will be the primary strategic challenge in these markets. Innovation will be the primary driver as markets mature and the level of customer sophistication rises. Shariah-compliant institutions will need to develop a process of product innovation to benefit from revenue of combined operations.

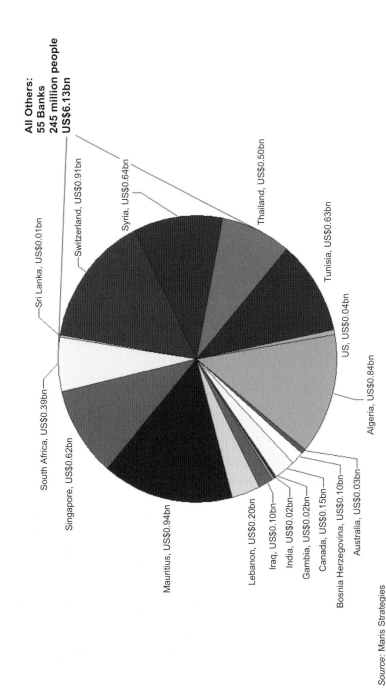

All Others:
55 Banks
245 million people
US$6.13bn

Switzerland, US$0.91bn

Syria, US$0.64bn

Thailand, US$0.50bn

Tunisia, US$0.63bn

Sri Lanka, US$0.01bn

US, US$0.04bn

Algeria, US$0.84bn

South Africa, US$0.39bn

Singapore, US$0.62bn

Mauritius, US$0.94bn

Lebanon, US$0.20bn

Iraq, US$0.10bn

India, US$0.02bn

Gambia, US$0.02bn

Canada, US$0.15bn

Bosnia Herzegovina, US$0.10bn

Australia, US$0.03bn

Source: Maris Strategies

Figure 4.3 Breakdown of Islamic Finance Industry's Smallest 1 Percentile

A Change in the Topology of Islamic Finance

Despite significant progress in recent years, Islamic financial institutions are still niche players in most of the marketplaces. As the market matures, fragmentation will increase due to new entrants and foreign multinational institutions seeking market share. As Islamic institutions grow, change their product mix, move into new geographies, alter their value proposition and continue to evolve their portfolio of services, there will be a gradual change in the topology of the market. Another factor that will reshape market topology is a growing concern that Islamic financial institutions, in their current state, are not capable of competing effectively with conventional financial institutions in terms of carrying out large transactions, cost-effective front to back office operations, and providing extensive branch networks to customers. An early sign of market consolidation is the merger between the Emirates Bank International and the National Bank of Dubai in October 2007, which brought together the UAE's second and fourth largest banks and created the largest bank in the Middle East by total assets, Emirates NBD. One factor that will frustrate the market is the difficulty in valuing assets in volatile times, which in turn will delay or postpone proposed mergers, such as happened in March 2009 when Bahrain's Ithmaar Bank delayed the proposed merger plan of its subsidiary Shamil Bank with the partly owned retail bank BBK.

An examination of the known 1,042 Shariah-compliant financial organizations reporting some type of business, banking or financial activity shows that the top 50 institutions comprise most of the market, as shown in Figure 4.4. The remaining approximately 1,000 financial organizations are relatively small, representing a highly fragmented industry, which, as the industry matures, will ultimately lead to a consolidation of market players.

In Malaysia, as the market for Shariah-compliant services expands to customers who are becoming more sophisticated in their demands for banking, finance and investment options, banks are beginning to cater to changes in attitudes driven by specific segments. For example, traditional Muslims are more comfortable with banks that are independently Shariah compliant and are less likely to bank with a conventional institution with an Islamic window. Thus from 2006 to 2009, several conventional banks with Islamic windows converted their operations to stand-alone Islamic banks. This was the case in November 2006, when CIMB Bank spun off its entire Islamic banking business to CIMB Islamic Bank. In early 2008, Maybank consolidated the Islamic window operations carried out by its subsidiaries and established an independent Maybank Islamic Bank. In

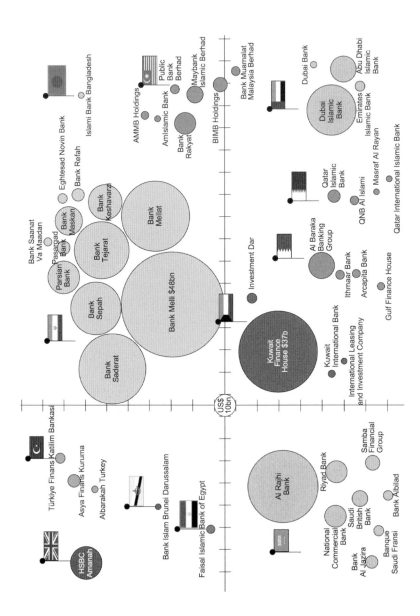

Figure 4.4 Relative Size Comparison of Top 50 Shariah-compliant Institutions by Asset Size

addition to this, Maybank went on an aggressive buying spree, spending some RM12 billion acquiring stakes in three banks: Vietnam's An Binh Commercial Joint Stock Bank, Pakistan's MCB Bank and Indonesia's Bank International Indonesia. However, as market conditions changed throughout 2008, Maybank Islamic Bank's merger attempt with Bank Islam was derailed when the central bank requested that stakeholders study their capital base more thoroughly in early 2009. Institutions in the Middle East have demonstrated a deliberate strategy for growth in terms of scale and scope through external acquisitions. There have been merger attempts between national players in order to consolidate operations, such as the discussion of a restructuring plan for a merger between Amlak Finance and Tamweel, two of the largest Islamic mortgage providers in the UAE. Clearly, Islamic financial institutions in the Middle East are extending their capabilities across geopolitical borders to increase market breadth. For example, in August 2008, Qatar National Bank acquired 24% of Commercial Bank International in Dubai. Another type of consolidation is the formation of "hybrid banks", demonstrated by National Bank of Kuwait's acquisition of a 40% stake of Boubyan Bank, which provided it with an Islamic window via Boubyan.

Perhaps the most underserved segment of the Islamic industry topology is that of microfinance and microbanking. Although vast numbers of Muslims live in the lower half of the economic pyramid, very little Shariah-compliant finance has yet to be extended into these populations. The total global outreach to Muslim customers reported by financial institutions is approximately 380,000 (80% from Indonesia, Bangladesh and Afghanistan), less than one-half of 1% of the estimated need for microfinance in Muslim communities.[25]

Transnational Market Interoperation

Just as people come together to form social networks, which are natural structures in society, financial institutions, government agencies, academic institutions and other support organizations are forming distinct networks within the known confines of what we now call Islamic finance. Sociologists understand that the formation of groups within society and organizations can reveal decision-making behaviour of a group or subgroup. This phenomenon is also taking place within the Islamic finance industry with the formation of groups interested in achieving homogeneity in Shariah-based regulatory structures, product identities and service descriptions. An oversimplification of the Islamic finance industry is depicted in Figure 4.5, which illustrates the three-tiered topology of the Islamic finance industry from the perspective of infrastructure development and the formation of support networks. As these networks form, innovation will play a significant role in defining the market depth (product innovation) and breadth (technological innovation for access to services). Perhaps the innovation that will have the most significant impact on these markets will be the development of intra-network transnational financial instruments designed to reduce liquidity shortfalls and surpluses between institutions.

To the casual observer, the Islamic finance industry appears to be highly fragmented with no central focus, yet, when viewed holistically, one can see the formation of transnational industry networks. The resulting networks are forming organically from rising needs in the industry, not from a design by a central authority. One such need is a recognized gap in the quality of professional financial services in Shariah-compliance issues. Responding to the gap in education, several institutions formed to provide the specific aspect of financial education. As the market matures, one can see the formation of an educational network that is focused on two immediate industry shortfalls: a lack of experienced Shariah scholars and a lack of high-quality financial services personnel.

Another network that is forming centres on issues of regulatory matters and improving the quality of the Shariah-compliant financial services industry, such as the formation of the Accounting and Auditing Organization for Islamic Financial Institutions (AAOIFI), whose mandate is to establish accounting and auditing standards. Additionally, a network of central bankers coupled with the formation of currency unions is addressing the synchronization of monetary, fiscal and economic policies, all of which have a direct impact on Islamic finance. One can also observe the formation of a capital markets network focusing on creating primary and secondary markets for Shariah-compliant financial instruments. As a network of banks reviews their appetite for mergers and acquisitions, there are several banks that are opting to collaborate in the establishment of a wide portfolio of products and services that can be white-labelled with other institutions.

Most networks are described as nodal, whereby each node on a network has a specific function connected by a telecommunications link, but what is forming in the Islamic finance industry is a non-nodal network similar to a human circulatory system. Unlike a traditional nodal network, the Islamic finance network is best described as a tubular network, in which monies and data "flow" between network members. In most cases, the flow is bidirectional with associated settlement processes to maintain the

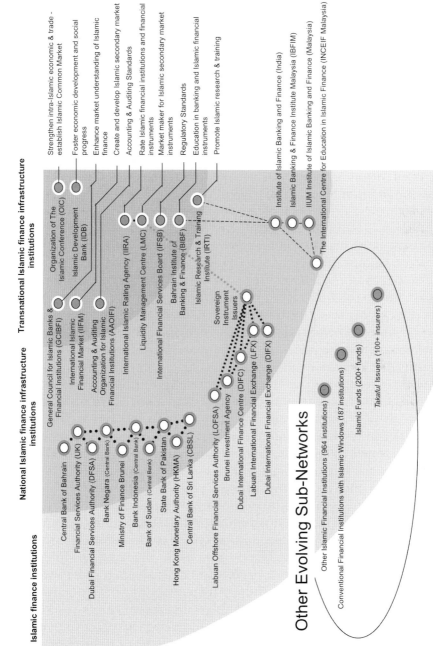

Islamic finance institutions

National Islamic finance infrastructure institutions

Transnational Islamic finance infrastructure institutions

- Central Bank of Bahrain
- Financial Services Authority (UK)
- Dubai Financial Services Authority (DFSA)
- Bank Negara (Central Bank)
- Ministry of Finance Brunei
- Bank Indonesia (Central Bank)
- Bank of Sudan (Central Bank)
- State Bank of Pakistan
- Hong Kong Monetary Authority (HKMA)
- Central Bank of Sri Lanka (CBSL)
- Labuan Offshore Financial Services Authority (LOFSA)
- Brunei Investment Agency
- Dubai International Finance Centre (DIFC)
- Labuan International Financial Exchange (LFX)
- Dubai International Financial Exchange (DIFX)

- General Council for Islamic Banks & Financial Institutions (GCIBFI)
- International Islamic Financial Market (IIFM)
- Accounting & Auditing Organization for Islamic Financial Institutions (AAOIFI)
- International Islamic Rating Agency (IIRA)
- Liquidity Management Centre (LMC)
- International Financial Services Board (IFSB)
- Bahrain Institute of Banking & Finance (BIBF)
- Islamic Research & Training Institute (IRTI)

- Organization of The Islamic Conference (OIC)
- Islamic Development Bank (IDB)

- Strengthen intra-Islamic economic & trade - establish Islamic Common Market
- Foster economic development and social progress
- Enhance market understanding of Islamic finance
- Create and develop Islamic secondary market
- Accounting & Auditing Standards
- Rate Islamic financial institutions and financial instruments
- Market maker for Islamic secondary market instruments
- Regulatory Standards
- Education in banking and Islamic financial instruments
- Promote Islamic research & training

- Sovereign Instrument Issuers

- Institute of Islamic Banking and Finance (India)
- Islamic Banking & Finance Institute Malaysia (IBFIM)
- IIUM Institute of Islamic Banking and Finance (Malaysia)
- The International Centre for Education in Islamic Finance (INCEIF Malaysia)

Other Evolving Sub-Networks

- Other Islamic Financial Institutions (964 institutions)
- Conventional Financial Institutions with Islamic Windows (187 institutions)
- Islamic Funds (200+ funds)
- *Takaful* Issuers (100+ insurers)

Figure 4.5 Islamic Finance Industry Topology

checks and balances of international capital flows. Tubular networks are radically different from other networks in terms of communication pathways, optimal structure and how the flow of capital is regulated.

Growth in the Islamic finance industry's network can be described as occurring in two distinctly different ways: exploratory and assimilative. Because of the lack of a robust financial infrastructure in many emerging nations, approximately 60% of the market's growth is exploratory, limited by the amount of capital that is applied to building infrastructure and capacity to service previously unbanked populations. Thus, the initial penetration into an emerging economy will be by international institutions that can provide their own infrastructure or simply extend their capabilities from a nearby region. The remaining 40% of the market's growth is assimilative, whereby connections between entities are increasing, as more Shariah-compliant financial service providers enter the market or establish relationships between themselves. As more institutions interact within a given region, the inherent resilience of the market increases because business activity is not reliant on the integrity of a single pathway. In economic terms, as more financial institutions become linked, their combined services within a market provide a greater number of higher quality financial instruments. For example, when financing the construction of a skyscraper, the source of funds along with the risk associated with providing the funds can be spread across a larger number of participating institutions and/or investors.

Assimilative growth increases connectivity within the network, allowing financial resources to circulate and be redistributed with greater frequency. It is important to remember that this evolving network of Islamic finance as an industry is self-integrating. Standardization becomes a vital component of the network – not to make all products look the same, but to provide mechanisms for banks, exchanges and markets to "plug in" to the network. Therefore, the growth of the industry and the associated innovation needed to fuel growth is directly proportional to the building of network relationships among infrastructure-oriented market providers, such as central banks, regulators, market makers, stock exchanges, banks, non-bank financial institutions, academic institutions and other providers of financial services such as payment networks. In other words, as more Shariah-compliant financial products enter the market providing greater choice to investors, the higher quality instruments will be recognized as preferred investments, while over time, poor performers will be withdrawn – Adam Smith's invisible hand of market dynamics is hard at work.

Infrastructure Institutions

Infrastructure is a broad term used by the industry to describe the regulations, operating structures, technology and ancillary support mechanisms needed to provide a nation with a safe, secure and solvent system of banking and finance. Within the scope of what can be classified as infrastructure are regulators, market makers, banks, educators and other support organizations. The role of the regulators is to enforce applicable laws, prosecute cases of market misconduct, license providers of financial services, protect clients, investigate complaints, and, perhaps most importantly, to maintain confidence in the financial system. Unlike other markets, Islamic finance is emerging as truly transnational, without any centrally organized authority multinational jurisdiction. Put simply, the markets are self-regulating by need not design. The following organizations have formed to play significant roles in the formation of the market and to assist in the overall development of the market for Islamic finance.

International Islamic Rating Agency

The Islamic International Rating Agency (IIRA) started operations in July 2005, working as an independent body within the financial services industry. The IIRA has a board of directors and an independent rating committee. Its Shariah board is composed of experts in the field. The purpose of the IIRA is to assist the Islamic financial services industry to gain recognition at a local and international level. The IIRA ensures that greater standards of disclosure and transparency are met, and it supports the development of the regional capital market.

Liquidity Management Centre

The Liquidity Management Centre (LMC) was established for the purpose of facilitating the investment of the surplus funds of Islamic banks and financial institutions into quality short- and medium-term financial instruments structured in accordance with Shariah principles. The LMC was formed by Bahrain Islamic Bank, Dubai Islamic Bank, Islamic Development Bank and Kuwait Finance House (each with 25% of its shares). The LMC plays a key role in the creation of an active and geographically expansive Islamic interbank market. This will assist Islamic financial institutions in managing their short-term liquidity.

Islamic Research and Training Institute

The Islamic Research and Training Institute (IRTI) was established in 1981 to undertake research and to provide both training and information services to Muslim communities to help them establish and maintain Shariah-compliant practices.

General Council for Islamic Banks and Financial Institutions
The General Council for Islamic Banks and Financial Institutions is an international autonomous non-profit corporate body. Its purpose is to represent Islamic banks and financial institutions and the Islamic financial industry globally. It is incorporated in the Kingdom of Bahrain.

Accounting and Auditing Organization for Islamic Financial Institutions
The Accounting and Auditing Organization for Islamic Financial Institutions (AAOIFI) was established in 1990. The AAOIFI is an Islamic international autonomous not-for-profit corporate body that prepares accounting, auditing, governance, ethics and Shariah standards for Islamic financial institutions and the industry.

To date, the development of these organizations has been purely due to industry need. As the industry continues to mature, the quality of products and services coupled with the capacity to process higher volumes will rise up the agenda of most financial institutions. The value of the infrastructure organizations is to enable the industry to self-assess and adjust its quality as it matures without the need for a central controlling body. The increased use of standards, synchronization of market offerings and the harmonization of Shariah principles all act to improve the overall quality of market offerings as well as provide higher levels of people and businesses using Shariah-compliant products. From a macroeconomic perspective in many nations, the aggregate effect is simple: more people and business moving from the informal economy into the formal economy. However, the transition between economic states within emerging economies coupled with the rapid growth and maturity rate of the Islamic finance industry raise numerous issues, as we will discuss in Chapter 5.

Notes

1   Barucci, P. (1985) A letter of credit drawn on the past, *UNESCO Courier*, February.

2   Farooq, M.O. (2006) Partnership, equity-financing and Islamic finance: whither profit-loss-sharing, Upper Iowa University, working paper, August, p. 14.

3   Vallely, P. (2006) How Islamic inventors changed the world, *The Independent* (London), March 11.

4   Brotton, J. (2003) *The Renaissance Bazaar: From the Silk Road to Michelangelo*, Oxford University Press, p. 46.

5 *Encyclopaedia Britannica*, 1911, Bill of exchange.

6 Hunt, E.S. and Murray, J.M. (1999) *A History of Business in Medieval Europe 1200–1550*, Cambridge University Press, p. 65.

7 Usmani, M.I.A. (2007) *A Guide to Islamic Banking (Gulf African Bank)*, Karachi, Darul Ishaat, p. 21.

8 Usmani, M.I.A., *A Guide to Islamic Banking*, p. 22.

9 Usmani, M.I.A., *A Guide to Islamic Banking*, pp. 22–3.

10 Usmani, M.I.A., *A Guide to Islamic Banking*, p. 24.

11 Usmani, M.I.A., *A Guide to Islamic Banking*, p. 26.

12 Irish, J. and Merzaban, D. (2009) Global crisis seen spurring Gulf Islamic finance, April 15, www.reuters.com/article/IslamicBankingandFinance09/idUSTRE53E4AA20090415.

13 Damak, M., Volland, E. and Maheshwari, R. (2009) *Sukuk* issuance fell dramatically in 2008 but long-term market prospects are good, Standard & Poor's Rating Direct Report, January 14, p. 2.

14 Taylor, J.B. (2004) Understanding and supporting Islamic finance: product differentiation and international standards, keynote address to the Harvard Islamic Finance Forum, Harvard University, May 8.

15 Shigehisa, K. (2002) The enigma of "time is money", *Japan Review*, **14**: 227.

16 Khan, W.M. (1989) Towards an interest-free Islamic economic system, *Journal of King Abdulaziz University Islamic Economics*, vol. 1, p. 4.

17 Gesell, S. (1929) *The Natural Economic Order*, Berlin, Neo-Verlag; Fisher, I. (1933) *Stamp Script*, New York, Adelphi; Keynes, J.M. (1936) *The General Theory of Employment, Interest and Money*, Macmillan.

18 DiVanna, J. (2008) A cloud is a promise, fulfilment is rain, *New Horizon*, January–March, 167.

19 Cited in DiVanna, J. (2008) A cloud is a promise, fulfilment is rain, *New Horizon*, January–March, 167, p. 22.

20 Creutz, H. (2001) *Das Geld Syndrom: Wege zu einer krisenfreien Marktwirtschaft*, Broschiert.

21 Fisher, I., *Stamp Script*.

22 Kennedy, M. (2004) Local currencies in the 21st century, paper presented at Bard College, New York, June 25–27, p. 6.

23 Fisher, I., *Stamp Script*.

24 Taing, A. (2009) Can Maybank digest another acquisition?, Malaysia, *The Edge*, February 23.

25 Karim, N., Tarazi, M. and Reille, X. (2008) Islamic microfinance: an emerging market niche, CGAP, Focus Note, Number 49, August, p. 1.

26 Adapted from Abdul Majid, Abdul Rais bin (2004) The role of international Islamic financial market in developing the international Islamic capital market, presentation at 1st Labuan International Islamic Finance Conference, July 6–7, p. 5.

5

INDUSTRY ISSUES IN CONTEXT

As the Islamic finance industry moves into its second generation of maturity, Shariah-compliant institutions will change their focus towards three types of innovation: new product design, streamlining internal business processes, and new technologies to increase access to services. Understandably, the underlying theme for this innovation on an industry scale is to increase the institutional capacity of Islamic finance. Strategically, financial institutions offering Shariah-compliant services are adopting strategies that foster new product development while protecting and strengthening their current competitive position. This implies that Islamic financial institutions will reassess their core competencies, capital structure, availability of funds, and compliance standards as competition for Shariah-compliant services increases as markets become saturated with new competitors.

Industry Issues and Strategies

Incumbent Islamic finance institutions must continually examine their underlying cost structure and rates of return to shareholders and depositors. Since Shariah-compliant institutions do not carry debt in the form of interest payments due to depositors, there will be increased pressure to assume additional risks to achieve profit expectations in line with other Islamic financial institutions and conventional banking competitors. Mergers and acquisitions, for example, will be part of larger Islamic financial institutions' strategy.

Strengthening the Islamic Financial System

At the heart of all financial systems is the understanding between an institution and a customer that a deposit (or investment) is the foundation from which a multitude of transactions are launched. Regulating the money flowing in and out of institutions is referred to as "liquidity", and its management is often more challenging in Islamic financial institutions. Put simply, liquidity is the convertibility of investments and other financial instruments into ready cash. To manage liquidity, Shariah-compliant institutions need to adopt a three-tiered banking system:

- Tier one acts as the foundation of the banking system as people put their money "in trust" with the institution via various savings and investment instruments.

- Tier two is analogous with mini-venture capital as funds from many people (sources) are combined under structures such as *mudarabah* to provide funding for business such as SMEs.

- The third tier resembles venture capital for larger investments such as infrastructure or project financing using *musharakah* structures.

Beyond the three-tiered system, interbank instruments are needed to channel excess liquidity between banks and other tools are needed to provide the industry with the fundamentals to manage liquidity.

Benchmarking

Benchmarking will play a significant role in the next generation of Islamic finance as institutions strive for greater efficiency. Measuring a Shariah-compliant organization against two independent benchmarks will be the key to gaining a competitive advantage. The first benchmark will be against international conventional banking best practices to evaluate an institution's relative efficiency and determine performance gaps. A second Islamic finance benchmark is necessary to determine overall performance relative to other Shariah-compliant institutions. One could argue that one benchmark is sufficient – that the measurement of Shariah-compliant institutions should be solely against their conventional counterparts. However, as the industry continues on its path of innovation, the assessment of the relative value of each innovation must be against similar competitive services. In a theoretical sense, as the industry develops products and services that are marginally different from their conventional counterparts, the current benchmarks will increasingly fall short of being a reliable indicator of relative performance.

To assess the health of a conventional US bank, regulators use the CAMELS rating: capital adequacy, asset quality, management, earnings, liquidity, and sensitivity to market risk. These five key factors are ranked on a scale of 1–5: 1 = strong, 2 = satisfactory, 3 = fair, 4 = marginal, and 5 = unsatisfactory. Banks with an average score of less than 2 are considered high-quality institutions, while banks with scores greater than 3 are considered less than satisfactory establishments. Lacking a central regulatory authority, the Islamic finance industry must rely on one of the emerging infrastructure support organizations to develop a mechanism similar to CAMELS, which could include other regional and transnational factors for assessing an institution's health. With no jurisdiction for enforcement of compliance, this rating system could be an indicator for senior management teams to reassess their operations. Externally, however, capital markets could use the mechanism to calculate their attitude towards a specific institution's stock price if publicly traded.

As the industry continues to mature, innovation is the key tool for accelerating the pace of implementing Islamic finance on the world stage. As we have discussed throughout this book, innovation has many forms and can be applied on many levels – from macroeconomic innovations such as currency unions and transnational settlement systems to microeconomic innovations such as peer-to-peer money transfers or microfinance. The rapid growth of the Islamic finance industry, coupled with movement up the industry maturity curve, presents senior managers at Shariah-compliant financial institutions with a number of industry issues. Managers must be aware that industry issues fall into two types of factor that must be part of their strategic planning process: factors outside their immediate control (external issues), and factors within their direct control (internal issues). When developing their competitive strategies, senior bankers must apply innovation to both sets of factors, using two different approaches for external and internal factors.

Strategic Thinking

One must consider the basic mechanism of strategy in order to assess the competitive relevance of numerous external and internal factors through a process that transforms a host of operating challenges into a set of single objective problems. External and internal factors are weighted and considered at various levels of a company's operating performance and reviewed through a set of changes in market conditions typically referred to as "scenarios". For Islamic financial institutions, the process of weighting each factor for relevance to the operating state of the organization introduces another level of communication between senior managers, the Shariah board and line managers. Numerous institutions are realizing the inefficiencies of their organizations when they develop their strategies in direct response to changes in the market. As the market for Islamic finance continues to grow, these organizational inefficiencies are magnified, creating a problem for the competitiveness of the institution.

Thus, senior management teams must turn to innovation to rethink their strategic planning process in order to keep pace with the industry as it matures. As the competition for Shariah-compliant services continues with the introduction of new providers of financial services, the process of how Islamic banks develop their strategies must be streamlined to accept input from many people in the organization and not simply be a process of deliberation between a few senior managers.

External Factors to be Considered Strategically

Senior management teams in financial institutions often delay or cancel projects that are focused on innovation due to external factors that cannot be adequately factored into the risk of taking a project forward. Put simply, uncertainty in financial markets fosters reserve; as a result, the confidence needed to move an innovation agenda forward is often lacking. Business plans to innovate new products, corporate strategies to expand market share and operational campaigns to move into new markets seem to have higher risks when external factors suddenly appear to have been underestimated. Management teams often classify external factors as threats when assessing their impact on their strategic intentions. External factors are often nation specific and categorized into four distinct groups: political, economic, social, and technological. An institution must assess the relevance of these dynamic factors against their strategic intentions. Once again, innovation must play a part as the dynamic nature of these factors demands that Shariah-compliant institutions revisit their strategies with greater frequency (in many cases monthly).

Political factors include political instability, risk of military invasion or military destabilization of a current government, the legal framework for contract enforcement, intellectual property protection, trade regulation and tariffs, favoured trading partners, anti-trust laws, pricing regulations, taxation (tax rates and incentives), wage legislation, working week, mandatory employee benefits, industrial safety regulations and product labelling requirements. These are increasingly becoming prime concerns of Islamic banking strategists due to their implications in product development. As Islamic finance continues its expansion across emerging market economies, political factors will play a bigger role in what products are offered in which countries, and under which conditions.

To date, innovation in the Islamic finance industry has been ahead of national governments' abilities to structure policy to impose boundaries on how the industry operates within tax regimes, regulatory frameworks and consumer protection guidelines. However, now that the industry has demonstrated that Shariah-based institutions are viable entities in the facilitation of financial services, the monitoring and control of the industry by local governments will increase. Once again, innovation will play a decisive role in influencing the growth rate of the industry. What most governments in emerging economies (and to some extent in industrialized economies such as the USA) have yet to realize is the political implications of how innovation in Islamic finance can be tied to political objectives such as economic development.

The second set of issues that senior managers must consider when developing strategic plans are economic factors such as the economic system of a nation state, the level of government intervention in the free market, comparative advantages of country, exchange rates and currency stability, and the efficiency of financial markets. Although these factors must be assessed in the context of how a Shariah-compliant institution sets its overall strategic objectives, there are other economic factors to be considered. These include infrastructure quality, skill level of workforce, labour costs, business cycle stage (for example prosperity, recession, recovery), economic growth rate, discretionary income levels, unemployment rate, inflation rate and interest rates (especially in non-Muslim or mixed economies where Shariah-compliant banks compete against conventional banks). Naturally, these economic factors have a great impact on specific plans to launch new products and services.

Perhaps the most significant set of issues that must be factored into the strategic plans of Shariah-compliant institutions are social factors such as demographics, class structure, education, culture (gender roles and so on), entrepreneurial spirit, attitudes (health, environmental consciousness, corporate social responsibility), and leisure interests. These factors drive how an institution structures Shariah-based products and services. Looking across the Islamic finance industry, we can see that social factors are rapidly changing in Muslim societies and are significantly different from one society to another. Upon closer examination, social factors within a national context reveal numerous variations in attitudes and varying degrees of social change among classes within Muslim societies, which can be used by an institution to drive the development of niche products. For example, the rising affluence of some Muslim women in countries such as the United Arab Emirates (UAE) has driven the development of women-only branches and women-only departments in Shariah-compliant banks.

The final set of issues that senior management teams must consider when setting their agenda for innovation within an institution are technological factors such as recent technological developments, technology's impact on product offering, cost structure and value chain structure, the rate of technological diffusion and technological adoption by customers. The influence of these factors cannot be underestimated because of the rising evidence of how technology is changing Muslim societies and how Muslim societies are changing technology. One key finding from conventional markets is that young people have the highest adoption rate of new technology, which is also true in Muslim societies. According to the United Nations Population Division, there are 1.5 billion people between the ages of 10 and 24.[1] If one reviews the demographics of Muslim societies, listed in Table 5.1, the vast majority of Muslim societies are relatively youthful.

In Middle East countries, young people (up to 24 years old) comprise the largest percentage of the population, for example Jordan 57.2%, Egypt 55.3% and Turkey 48.3%.[2] Young people and their approach to using technology will be an external factor that will increasingly influence the strategies of Shariah-compliant institutions. Technology adoption within a banking context depends on the technology, what services are facilitated by its use and the context in which it is used. With the rising youth culture in nations where Islamic finance provides services, how banking, investment and other financial services are delivered will be at the fore-front of the retail banking agenda. Strategically, as the youth culture matures, the impact of how they use technology to facilitate business will influence corporate banking services and investment banking. Mobile telephony is changing young people's lifestyles and attitudes towards the convenience of banking services. Throughout the Muslim world, young people who consider themselves technologically savvy are changing how banks define themselves. It is clear that when banks develop their strategic initiatives, each external factor must now be weighted higher than internal factors against short-term and long-term agendas. This is not to say that external factors have a higher overall value, but it does mean that external factors will influence the short-term and long-term agendas differently, because senior management teams cannot exercise the same level of influence over external factors as they can over the internal capabilities of the organization. The key learning is that external factors often change the long-term strategic intent because they dictate to the institution elements of value that are often counterintuitive.

Table 5.1 Age Comparison of Predominately Muslim Nations to Several Industrialized Nations						
Country	Number of Muslims (in millions)	Muslim percentage of population	Median age	Population growth rate percentage (2009 est.)	Birth rate per 1,000 (2009 est.)	Percentage of population under age 15
Indonesia	204	88	27.6	1.136	18.84	28.1
Pakistan	164	97	20.8	1.947	27.62	37.2
India	154	14	25.3	1.548	21.76	31.1
Bangladesh	128	83	23.3	1.292	24.68	34.6
Turkey	76	99	27.7	1.312	18.66	27.2
Egypt	74	94	24.8	1.642	21.7	31.4
Nigeria	73	75	19.0	1.999	36.65	41.5
Iran	65	98	27.0	0.882	17.17	21.7
Morocco	34	98	25.0	1.479	20.96	30.0
Algeria	33	99	26.6	1.196	16.90	25.4
Afghanistan	32	99	17.6	2.629	45.46	44.5
Saudi Arabia	28	100	21.6	1.848	28.55	38.0
Sudan	28	85	19.1	2.143	33.74	40.7
Iraq	27	97	20.4	2.507	30.1	38.8
Ethiopia	27	65	16.9	3.208	43.66	46.1
United States	2.3	0.8	36.7	0.975	13.82	20.2
United Kingdom	1.6	2.7	40.2	0.279	10.65	16.7
Germany	4.4	4.9	43.8	−0.053	8.18	13.7
Japan	0.1	0.09	44.2	−0.191	7.64	13.5

The Basis for Strategic Understanding

Where innovation plays a major role in how a Shariah-compliant institution comes to market, develops products or builds new capacity, the key to developing competitive strategies is to prioritize external factors according to their direct and indirect impact on the financial institution's strategic intentions. Senior managers must use external factors as the first means of prioritizing their strategic initiatives. It is important to understand how each factor influences the overall strategic plan. If one considers the relative size of Shariah-compliant institutions to their conventional counterparts, this process of prioritization is critical, due to the limited resources of the institution, as indicated in Table 5.2.

The key learning for senior managers is that external factors are the first consideration when considering strategic objectives. When considering external factors in this context, their greatest influence is on future operating states. In most cases, external factors do not change quickly – they occur over many months or years. The timing and weight of external factors have varying effects on people's financial behaviours, for example attitudes towards savings and borrowing change over generations, while the timing of external factors, such as political instability, may be unpredictable.

External Factors Create Challenges and Opportunities

There are a number of external factors that industry analysts have noted as prime obstacles to the next wave of growth in Islamic finance. As an industry, the shortfalls in national financial infrastructure, such as the lack of uniform standards of credit analysis across Islamic banking markets, limit the rate at which Shariah-compliant institutions can finance individuals and small businesses. Although the call from market analysts is for an appropriate standard of credit analysis, the establishment of national standards or the creation of credit rating agencies are both steps towards resolving this problem. Along similar lines is the need to train the banking personnel in Shariah-compliant banks, not only to achieve a more comprehensive understanding of Shariah principles, but also to develop a deeper knowledge of how to apply products to customers' lifestyles.

Macroeconomics

On a macroeconomic scale, there are factors such as the relationship between a Shariah-compliant financial institution and the central bank. Islamic banks have been established as separate legal entities, therefore their relationship with central banks and/or other commercial banks is

Table 5.2 Example of Strategy Worksheet to Weight External Factors

Strategic objective	Realization	External factors				Key factor (factor with highest weight)
		Political	Economic	Social	Technological	
Expand into new market	Establish single branch as pilot	Government pro Islamic finance, cautious about being seen as promoting a religious agenda	Economy growing at 2.3%, GDP at 2.1%, Muslims populations are in the lower half of the economic pyramid	45% of Muslim population under 25 years old, rising middle class, 32% of secondary education graduates attend university	Mobile phone adoption rate at 400,000 new subscribers per year, internet penetration at 3% of total population, national ATM network at 2,300	Two Shariah-compliant banks are offering basic banking services, less than 10% of Muslim population served, most Muslims do not have access to any banking
Expand product portfolio	Pilot new product (Shariah-compliant credit card) with a target segment	Review regulatory issues and understand general consensus on card from Shariah scholars' point of view	Market analysis identifies 349,000 potential customers, total cards issued in country is 14,500	The issue of *riba* must be clear to the customer, as well as the utility of the card	Only 8% of population uses cards, educating customers will be a factor	Must address the social attitude towards credit cards and assess the value of packaging cards into 3–4 offerings
Expand product per customer	Increase the cross-sell ratio of products	Concern over our debt products and consumers getting into financial trouble	Product penetration in local market is 2.1 per customer US market is 5.5	Customers are risk adverse with an increasing appetite for debt-like products	Use branch as a means to educate customers and migrate them to internet, mobile and ATM channels	Develop link between each factor and its potential impact on the cost/income ratio
Repackage and restructure products to reflect changing consumer lifestyles	Develop product linkages and product migration strategy	Consumer advocacy groups complaining about fees and rates	Lifestyle metrics reveal that during the crisis the middle class needs to reorganize its total debts	People living beyond their means will pay a premium to restructure their overall debt over longer terms	Develop customer/debt profiling tool on internet for customers to prequalify	Develop clear definitions of lifestyle metrics to perform product matching

not often clear when considering the provisioning of short-term invest-ment instruments. This issue, although not resolved in Islamic nations, is exacerbated in non-Muslim markets. Once again, innovation by central bankers and commercial banks has to play a significant role in resolving these issues by working with Shariah scholars to develop high-quality, short-term instruments with appropriate credit ratings and liquidity.

In non-Muslim nations, the revision of tax regimes to meet the needs of Islamic products is needed to create a level playing field with conven-tional products. Disclosure requirements must be more comprehensive and the frequency that institutions inform investors of the investment techniques, structures and methods of financing must be constructed in such a way that customers can make informed decisions based on their risk preference. Transparency and adequate disclosure of Shariah-compliant financing mechanisms are vital in building the foundation for Islamic finance.

According to Taylor, there must be an international effort to design a regulatory framework for Islamic finance, whereby regulators take into consideration the factors and differences found in Shariah-compliant financing and devise minimal standards or benchmarks to gauge comp-liance and assess risks.[3] Taylor rightly points out the need for consistency in regulatory treatment across the board, subject to the particular coun-try's legal and regulatory regime. Recognition of national statutes and the synchronization of the enforcement of these laws by the relevant national regulators demonstrate forward progress on establishing internationally accepted regulatory standards to address the issues of regional interpreta-tion of Shariah compliance.

Economic policies

One role of economic policy is to establish an environment consisting of a regulatory framework and tax structure with incentives to promote innov-ation in financial markets. Regulatory frameworks should demonstrate the proper controls on activities to build investor confidence, while not imposing a high cost or excessive burden on businesses. To date, the regulatory frameworks and tax structures in Muslim nations have been advantageous to the growth of Islamic finance, developing the pace at which the industry increases its market depth and breadth. As a result of liberal national economic policies and the broad remit given to Shariah-compliant institutions, a diversified range of Islamic financial products and services has emerged to effectively mobilize financial resources that meet the investment requirements of the economy. Consequently, the vast majority of institutional products are basic Islamic transactions repackaged to reflect conventional financial instruments with the non-Shariah-compliant elements removed.

As the industry enters the next generation of growth, innovation will take on a new role in product development. As new regulatory and supervisory standards emerge across nations, the composition of innovations will have to incorporate a larger number of variables. This progression into the next generation of products will reflect a greater diversity of Shariah interpretation, as the industry moves from providing basic banking and investment services to address the new demands of increasingly sophisticated Islamic investors.

Regulations and the central banks
Banking is an industry of managed risks. Although the media portrays banking in the economic climate of 2008–09 as a risky business, banking in general is a process of assessing and mitigating numerous risk-laden factors. Islamic banks assess and mitigate risks in the same way as other financial institutions, in addition to the process of risk sharing imposed by Shariah principles. Thus, risk management within Shariah-compliant financial institutions is a process that identifies, assesses, manages, monitors and mitigates potential risks within the institution's capacity and capital adequacy requirements. Therefore, the range of risks differ in nature from those borne by commercial banks, as Shariah compliance requirements combine with those of the various local/regional regulatory requirements and the emerging international standards of BASEL II.

As the Islamic finance industry continues to mature with innovation playing a larger part in the overall growth of the market, the role of central banks and various regulatory agencies will change to reflect the supervisory needs of new products. Principally, in the aftermath of the credit crisis, the regulators are being scrutinized, as popular sentiment moves from initial outrage to a search for people and organizations responsible for the global economic downturn. Unfortunately, in this economic drama, regulators are being portrayed as financial guardians who fell asleep on their watch. As a result, regulators worldwide will increase their vigilance in monitoring the financial industry, and if history is any guide to regulatory behaviour, they will overreact to market conditions to take an ultraconservative posture in financial oversight. Regulators in Muslim countries and their counterparts in other economies must ensure that they restructure their roles in the avoidance of economic problems related to the financial industry in order to enable innovation to occur further.

Transborder Islamic finance is one area that will receive renewed attention from regulators, as Shariah-compliant financial institutions look beyond their traditional borders to expand their operations. Just as the Accounting and Auditing Organization for Islamic Financial Institutions (AAOIFI), the Islamic Financial Services Board (IFSB) and others act to facilitate industry-wide standards, regulators and central banks must come together to establish regional guidelines on how Islamic finance will interact with national regulatory structures. Consequently, as regulators become more adept at understanding new Shariah-compliant innovations, the Islamic finance industry will undergo regulatory synchronization.

The risk assessment process used by Shariah-compliant institutions will receive special attention from regulators, as the nature of risks faced by Islamic banks is somewhat different from conventional institutions in terms of assets and inventory assessment, investment costs, regular income and recognition of losses, and adequacy of guarantees. The dilemma for regulators will be the development of mechanisms to cover such risks while encouraging competition and market innovation.

A Taxing Matter

The first generation of Islamic finance has enjoyed substantial growth in relatively tax-free environments, with a few exceptions such Malaysia and the UK. After numerous discussions on Islamic finance, the UK government moved to revise taxation laws to address key issues such as double taxation, which occurs when Islamic banks purchase real estate on behalf of their customers and sell the asset back to the customer. Pakistan's government incorporated a general provision to exempt Islamic finance from taxation on a cross-border basis; however, there were no specific provisions for Shariah-compliant products within the country.

Perhaps an oversimplification of the tax issue is the treatment of tax on interest and capital gains on ordinary citizens. Under conventional tax regimes such as in the USA, interest acquired by an individual is taxed as income. US tax regulations also have provisions for tax credits on some forms of interest paid, such as mortgage interest. Thus, Muslim customers in the USA would be disadvantaged over other citizens when they seek Shariah-compliant home financing, because the amount they pay for financing (which is not considered mortgage interest) is not considered tax deductible. Therefore, Muslims living under similar tax regimes are penalized for practising their faith, not because they are Muslims, but because antiquated tax codes reflect the American ethos of home ownership, which over decades has resulted in a tax code that favours the banks charging interest.

Similar tax treatment issues exist for financial institutions in nations such as the UK, where, in conventional terms, interest payments made by banks to depositors are deductible from gross income before taxes are calculated. Shariah-compliant institutions offering deposit accounts that pay a share of profits are not deductible because the payment is considered as the distribution of profit or dividends. The semantic difference between the two types of payments from banks to depositors highlights the fact that tax codes in non-Muslim countries may hinder the overall growth of Shariah-compliant market until provisions are negotiated.

Although innovation in taxation sounds like an oxymoron, as Islamic finance moves into non-Muslim nations or nations with tax regimes that are the remnants of European colonialism, tax codes will have to be renegotiated to enable Shariah-compliant financial institutions to compete viably with their conventional counterparts.

Standardization and Market Harmonization

Industry analysts critical of Islamic finance often point out that a lack of global standards in Shariah compliance is the industry's Achilles heel. Conventional markets need financial product standardization to integrate various instruments, interoperate across national economies, reduce market inefficiencies, build consumer confidence and establish benchmarks that enable comparisons of similar financial structures. The logic behind the need for standards is the underlying need to promote stability in financial markets. However, standards did little to prevent the collapse of banking systems globally during the financial crisis of 2008–09. In fact, one could argue that standardization and the ability to integrate financial products helped to facilitate the speedy implosion of the world's financial systems. Nevertheless, over the long term, standards are good for market growth and financial stability. Within Islamic finance, organizations such as the AAOIFI, the IFSB, the General Council for Islamic Banks and Financial Institutions, the Islamic International Rating Agency and the Fiqh Academy in Jeddah are at the vanguard of standards' innovation as they work to align Shariah principles in an industry that is growing as fast as standards can be written.

As the market for Shariah-compliant financial products continues to evolve, the need for market harmonization will continue to grow, although in the early days of the second generation of Islamic finance, the use of some product structures may not hold up to long-term scrutiny. Among Shariah scholars, there is and will continue to be healthy debate on the validity of certain contracts within the different schools of thought. It is possible that complete harmonization is neither achievable nor desirable because of the limitations on how scholars could interpret Shariah principles, and this requires some leeway in the application of principles during the process of market innovation.[4] At the heart of the debate is the use of structures that are seen as Shariah compliant under one interpretation and not fully compliant under another, for example the use of *bai inah and bai al dayn* structures by East Asian Muslims, which Middle East Muslims see as being not fully compliant. In the Malaysian context, structures such as *bai inah* (sell and buy back contract), *bai bithaman ajil* (deferred payment sale contract) and *bai al dayn* (debt trading contract) fill a market need for financing that is fundamentally different due to the demographic composition of the nation. The needs of microfinance, such as the fact that poor people rarely have assets they can sell or capitalize, create a condition in which a scholar must interpret Shariah principles to best fit the needs of the local community and the individuals involved. When reviewing financial structures out of context, the practice seems to reflect a fragmented industry with a modicum of standardized practices. However, when placed in their original context, the interpretive nature of how scholars apply Shariah principles to facilitate commerce in a way that preserves Islamic ideals, such as fair and equitable treatment between parties, is, indeed, the hidden strength of Islamic financial innovation.

Factors Internal to the Institution

In the realm of internal institutional factors, the vast majority of financial institutions including Shariah-compliant institutions have a formal process of strategic planning. Typically, this process is top down, whereby executives periodically formulate the strategic intentions of the organization and then communicate these intentions down to the organization for implementation. Depending on the size of the financial institution, executive teams have two organizing philosophies:

- larger institutions manage a portfolio of business activities of business units looking for synergies and opportunities for mergers or acquisitions

- smaller institutions focus their attentions on direct ways to improve the overall performance of their operations.

In both cases, a company's capabilities are compared with its capacity, which are in turn considered in the context of competitive threats and opportunities.

Perhaps the most notable change in innovation is the shift from using technology to gain organizational efficiencies to supporting a growth agenda. This is not to say that innovation is not being used as a means to gain process efficiencies within the organization, merely that senior management teams now realize that cost reductions cannot be the prime objective of innovation. In turn, innovation must be applied to leveraging an organization's capabilities to achieve its corporate objectives. The capabilities inherent in the organization must be leveraged to do more with less, such as increase the volume of transactions without increasing the number of staff. Senior management teams are evaluating innovation under a new set of criterion, such as: can we achieve a 40% growth in customers and a 15% growth in transaction volume by applying innovation to existing processes?

The capabilities and capacity of the organization to generate shareholder value while maintaining profitable operations in the current and future business climate is the primary concern when considering a host of factors within the control of the executive management team. In the rapidly changing economic climate, the process of developing top-down strategies has one inherent flaw – it was designed for stable economic environments where competition was well defined and unexpected events are rare. Shariah-compliant institutions must once again use innovation to rethink the fundamental process of strategic thinking, especially when considering how external factors impact an organization's competitive abilities.

Brand Development

A financial institution's brand is a strategic asset, and Shariah-compliant institutions are beginning to realize that they must be proactive in managing the brand of the firm in the same way they manage any other asset. In a classical context, strong brands deliver better business performance while decreasing acquisition cost, because customers become repeat buyers.[5] Shariah-compliant financial institutions are becoming more aware of the value of their brands as the markets they serve continue to mature. Providers of Islamic finance focusing on high net worth customers have learned that they are willing to pay a premium for services with a strong brand identity because of the implied quality or appearance of significant growth of the institution.

However, brand management is a relatively new, often misunderstood concept among Shariah-compliant financial institutions. Senior management teams that realize the value of brand development are also discovering that the process of creating and managing a brand identity is often beyond their in-house capabilities. This is not to say that they lack the ability to effectively design, launch and manage their brand identities. What is clear is that external intervention is needed to examine the brand holistically in the context of being relevant to numerous customer types. That is, external brand consultants see the brand in the context of the other brands competing for the same customers. The real value of external brand consultants is that they provide an external perspective of the market and the customer, which is often difficult for internal teams.

One of the most successful launches of a Shariah-compliant financial institution was the London launch of Gatehouse Bank in 2008. As the bank was focused on achieving its authorization from the Financial Services Authority and building strong front and back office teams, it was logical to find a partner that could help it create an effective plan and then execute it. Gatehouse selected the Madano Partnership (a communications consultancy) to allow it to stay focused on the activities that added most value, while controlling costs.[6] Gatehouse realized that innovation is not always about a big new idea (although the bank's positioning was entirely new), but in combining a myriad of details and faultless execution. The key lesson learned was to define specific target audiences and deliver concise, well-scripted messages. This was an innovative approach in an industry that often tries to connect with everyone.

A launch phase requires a broad range of skills, but also requires the ability of the project team to flex capacity as required to deliver all the required deliverables and activities. Again, by outsourcing, Gatehouse ensured it had the right skills and capacity to drive its marketing communications. Prepared with a clear set of business objectives, Gatehouse needed to define a brand and communications strategies that would set it apart from the competition in the competitive London marketplace. Gatehouse is not a retail bank, but a wholesale investment bank focused on bridging the western and Middle Eastern markets from the heart of the City of London's emerging market for Shariah-compliant financial services. As a City investment bank, Gatehouse is an ultraprofessional organization and this had to be brought to life and communicated in all its branding and media interactions. Its focus also defines its key target audiences, which helped to shape its communications plan and activities

Gatehouse's aspirations are to facilitate financial deals on a global basis, so the initial focus was on international publications and the internet. Its strategy was to agree to supply exclusive stories with non-competitive international publications, reinforced with precise advertising. Coupled with optimising its website for continual updates and search engines, Madano's Gatehouse campaign was able to grow the number of people looking for Gatehouse or its related services month on month. This route was vindicated as Gatehouse Bank was voted Best New Islamic Bank in the world for 2008 in *Islamic Finance News'* respected annual awards. Clearly, this was primarily down to the bank itself, but its launch had created a powerful global impact.

Liquidity Management

Liquidity management has become an area of increasing concern among executive management teams, regulators, shareholders and industry analysts. The liquidity of Shariah-compliant institutions could be managed through the interbank fund market by direct placement in case of surplus to be used by other institutions in need of liquidity, that is, excess funds from one bank can be loaded to another bank in search of additional funds. In conventional markets, this is common practice, with banks using an interbank lending rate (interest). However, this type of interest-based lending is not appropriate for Shariah-compliant banks so an alternative mechanism has to be developed. Numerous market entities are experimenting with new innovative approaches to address this shortfall; however, no preferred mechanism has become the standard. *Mudarabah* is the most applicable instrument in this case. Another way is through securitization of well-performing assets, for example buying *sukuk* at par at the time of issue, holding them and earning rental or profit, then in case of need (short of liquidity), selling them into the secondary market to generate cash. If *sukuk* are not available, another method is to develop a portfolio of *murabahah* or *ijarah* assets and invite other Shariah-compliant banks to invest. Also in cases of liquidity, deficit cash could be generated through parallel *salam* contracts.

The issue of liquidity is so prominent that the Liquidity Management Centre (LMC) was established by Bahrain Islamic Bank, Dubai Islamic Bank, Islamic Development Bank and Kuwait Finance House to assist Shariah-compliant banks to manage their liquidity in both surplus and deficit requirements. The LMC attracts assets internationally and from the public as well as the private sector and securitizes them into securities that are more available. It also provides short-term liquid Treasury assets in the form of *sukuk* for various Shariah-compliant firms to invest their surplus.[7]

Managing Risk

A 2007 IMF study of 77 Islamic banks in 20 countries ascertained that Islamic financial institutions have a higher degree of stability than conventional banks, with smaller Islamic institutions having the highest degree of stability.[8] In the IMF's view, one explanation is that as Islamic institutions grow in scale, their ability to manage the complexity of their various profit/loss arrangements is limited by their systems to monitor/manage effectively their credit risk. Thus, as an Islamic institution grows, the problems of adverse selection and moral hazard become greater as the number of agreements rise. Another factor brought up by the IMF survey centred on the degree to which smaller Islamic institutions concentrated on lower risk investments and fee income, which differentiates them from their larger counterparts that focus more on profit and loss sharing.

Risks unique to Islamic banks arise from the specific features of Islamic contracts, and the overall legal, governance and liquidity infrastructure of Islamic finance, as Čihák and Hesse argue.[9] In profit and loss-sharing contracts, the direct credit risk shifts from the banks to the investors (depositors). This also increases the overall degree of risk of the asset side of banks' balance sheets, because it makes Islamic banks vulnerable to risks normally borne by equity investors rather than holders of debt. In addition, because of compliance with Shariah law, Islamic banks can use fewer risk-hedging techniques and instruments (such as derivatives and swaps) than conventional banks. The risks within an Islamic bank are operational risks, credit, security and fraud risks, among many others. The issue here is that risk, in the context of key challenges facing Islamic banks for the next 10 years, falls into two broad categories: operational risk and reputational risk.

Operational risk can be defined as the risk of monetary losses resulting from inadequate or failed internal processes, people and systems, or from external events.[10] Differentiating between external and internal losses is key, because external losses are more easily defined – such as natural disasters and other factors that interrupt the business, which are, for the most part, beyond the organization's control. Internal losses, such as a loss of market confidence (a component of reputational risk), employee fraud, product flaws, breaches in security and other internal problems, are more difficult to define and allay due to their complexity. The mitigation of external risks is often reactive, with a great deal of pre-planning in disaster recovery plans that are activated after the event has occurred. In a vast number of banking institutions, the internal mitigation process is also reactive, a flaw or problem develops and the firm harnesses resources to

resolve the problem. The same structural problems exist in Islamic institutions with the added complexity of Shariah compliance, legal risk and
the awareness of local cultural idiosyncrasies of Muslim customers. In an
Islamic bank, the degree of risk is often compounded because of the profit
and loss-sharing agreements. The key to long-term viability for Shariah-
compliant institutions will be to become proactive in addressing structural
problems within the bank.

Structural problems emerge as a by-product of business processes that
do not adjust themselves to changes in the operating environment. Banks
establish clear, well-defined business processes complete with operating
procedures supported by multimillion-dollar investments in computer
hardware and software. However, even with increasing levels of business
process computerization, the origination and servicing of numerous
customized product offerings (deals) are, in many cases, fulfilled manually
on paper. Structural flaws are magnified when institutions grow or when
they are merged with another bank.

Is bigger better?

Čihák and Hesse's examination of the financial stability of Islamic banks
noted that smaller Islamic banks tend to be financially stronger than their
conventional counterparts and larger Islamic banks.[11] In Čihák and Hesse's
view, this is because of the discipline that focuses them on low-risk and
fee income activities unlike their larger counterparts that concentrate
more on profit and loss-sharing business. This brings into context another
challenge for Islamic institutions, which is a matter of scale; at what point
do Islamic banks become less efficient and more susceptible to risk?

Risk is traditionally lower in Islamic institutions because of the nature
of their operating philosophies and their attitude towards financing.
Theoretically, as smaller institutions merge, they achieve greater efficiencies through the consolidation of business processes and administrative
functions. In the case of Islamic banks, this may not be entirely true, as
the additional complexity creates suboptimal processes and increased
levels of documentation needed to support Shariah compliance objectives.
One caveat to this line of thinking is that, in industry terms, Islamic
banking is still relatively immature compared with conventional banking
and as institutions gain experience in leveraging technology to solve
operational problems, the scaling problem may subside.

Risk and market discipline

In times of economic growth, Islamic bank depositors set their return on
investment expectations slightly higher than their conventional counter-

parts because of their perceptions of shared risk and shared return. Often the shared risk is not clearly understood or perhaps conveniently misunderstood when banks underperform against those expectations. Customers are disappointed when they discover that they are contractually obligated to help to absorb losses. Thus, to avoid alienating customers, Islamic banks protect customer investments using two types of reserves, which act as shock absorbers when investments perform below expectations: profit equalization reserves and displaced commercial risk reserves. Profit equalization reserves are designed to provide assurance that anticipated profit expectations can be maintained for customers. Displaced commercial risk reserves are used to offset severe losses. In most cases, banks are unwilling to use customer funds to cover losses. Thus, Shariah-compliant structures like *mudarabah* and *wakalah* funds provide a partial buffer to absorb losses for customers.[12] The possibility of catastrophic loss has led regulators to instruct banks to hold capital against some portion of the assets in which their *mudarabah* and *wakalah* accounts are invested.[13]

Asset Class Diversification

Like their non-Muslim counterparts, Muslim investors seek to diversify their portfolios to mitigate risks. During the first generation of Islamic financial innovation, investments in real estate, equities, gold and silver offered varying degrees of investment diversification, but fell short of investor demand for Shariah-compliant investments. As demand has grown over the past five years, financial institutions began to innovate in several markets such as Bahrain, Malaysia and the UAE, bringing Shariah-compliant stocks, mutual funds, private equity funds, unit trusts and exchange traded funds to markets. However, not all innovations have met with equal enthusiasm; the introduction of Islamic hedge funds failed to attract sufficient numbers of investors to make them viable due to their relatively small size and cost. Much of the innovation and market appeal for Islamic finance has been centred on the ethical soundness of an investment. As we move into the next generation of product diversification, innovation will have to be applied taking into consideration the financial appeal of the products to investors.

Better Understanding of the Balance Sheet

In the decade prior to the meltdown of the financial markets in 2008, the vast majority of investors laboured under the misconception that they did not have time to read or understand a corporation's financial accounts, and that it was simpler to leave that task to professional fund managers. Financial advisers realized that few investors take the time to read and understand the balance sheet and income statement of a bank, and even fewer investors understand how to interpret the financial accounts of a Shariah-compliant institution. However, now investors are attempting to understand a corporation's financial accounts. This poses a new challenge for Shariah-compliant institutions, as how their operations and actions are recorded in financial statements is not consistent across the industry. Therefore, potential investors in Islamic finance must have some know-ledge of the structural nuances brought about by Shariah compliance. The way accounts are structured reflects the nature of Shariah-compliant banks as intermediaries, with the ratio of capital to liabilities representing a fundamentally different approach to the management of risk and an adherence to a driving set of ethical ideals.[14]

Human Capital in Islamic Finance

Shariah principles are the underlying foundation of Islamic banking and finance. Although these principles are based on two primary sources, the Holy Qur'an and the Sunnah, their broad application varies from region to region. To conventional bankers, global investors and various Islamic groups, the inconsistency in the application of Shariah principles can be seen as a weakness in the Islamic banking system. However, the variability found in the interpretations is the strength of Islamic banking in the adaptability of the principles to many societies that make up the *ummah* (nation). During the first generation of Islamic finance, bankers worked with Shariah scholars to design products in an iterative fashion. Financial institutions brought products to the market and customers embraced the new products for a wide variety of reasons. Bankers understood banking and Shariah scholars understood how to interpret Shariah principles and apply them to financial intermediation.

As the industry matures and customers' needs become more sophistic-ated, simply being a banker is no longer sufficient; bankers need a broad base of knowledge of how to apply Shariah-compliant products to best fit the variations in lifestyles of Muslims. Thus, a gap in human capital at all levels within Shariah-compliant institutions is increasing – as the popul-arity of the industry grows, there are now not enough bankers with the appropriate skills. Moreover, the lack of Shariah scholars with an in-depth knowledge of financial products has become a constraining factor in several markets. These two gaps in human capital are a symptom of an industry experiencing growing pains. To keep pace with the market demand for Shariah-compliant finance, innovation has to play a role in reconfiguring the overall problem. The establishment of Shariah databases to provide scholars with a central repository of *fatwa* (a scholarly opinion on a matter of Islamic law) knowledge has been proposed as a national resource. Technology will provide new tools for the education of the next generation of Shariah scholars. The innovative aspect of these technologies is to give new scholars a holistic understanding of Shariah principles and their subsequent *fatwas* in the context of how they are applied to various financial transactions and the circumstances surrounding the transactions. However, applying technology to Shariah scholarship is not intended to codify Shariah interpretation but to provide scholars with the tools to analyse and identify compliance problems, which are a result of insufficient policies and procedures within a Shariah-compliant institution.

Cost Control and Bank Efficiency

Muslim and non-Muslim customers alike have noticed that when compared with their conventional counterparts, Islamic finance is often more expensive than conventional finance. This perception, whether real or imagined, has an impact on a bank's ability to attract and retain customers. Therefore, to be competitive, Shariah-compliant institutions must address every aspect of their underlying cost structure in an effort to streamline their operations. Islamic institutions can charge commission or fees for services rendered (*ujr*). These fees do not represent a payment of interest, rather, they are allowable expenses incurred by the institution in the delivery of specific services to customers, or they reflect the cost of operating under structures like *mudarabah*. That said, when customers are comparing fees based on value for money, the market perception is that Muslims are assessed a premium for practising their beliefs. Therefore, banks must clearly describe the costs associated with their products to avoid customer confusion. Likewise, banks must diligently lower their cost structures and build marketing credibility on the quality of their products to penetrate global markets.

According to Mohamed Ariff, the average Islamic bank generates only 87.9% of its profit potential, which delivers 13.8% more profits than using comparable resources in a conventional bank.[15] In Ariff's view, Islamic banks have ample room to improve both their cost efficiency and profit efficiency. Analysis of Islamic banks by size indicates that new institutions are more efficient at generating profits. Therefore, achieving scale is a problem within Islamic institutions and is one area that banks need to innovate. The efficiency of a Shariah-compliant institution is measured by how close a bank comes to earning maximum profit, given its output level. When calculating the efficiency ratio of Islamic institutions, two factors must be taken into account: interest expenses are replaced with profits distributed to depositors, and the depreciation value should include the depreciation in physical capital that is bought for leasing.[16]

The number of studies on the efficiency of Shariah-compliant institutions is small when compared with research on conventional banking efficiency, but it will continue to develop in depth and breadth.[17]

Documentation and the Cost of Compliance

To ensure the fidelity of Shariah compliance, Islamic banks have a propensity to be document intensive. Characteristically, transactions have a series of phases such as contract, procurement, sale, financing and servicing, in which a plethora of documents are required at various stages of the transaction. Completing all the documentation at once may render the transaction void or *haram*, because the "elapse of time" between the stages is sometimes essential to the acceptance of the structure itself, for example *tawarruq*. One key challenge for Islamic institutions is to streamline their internal process and automate as much documentation as is practically possible. Documents can be codified and evidence of the elapse of time can be monitored to meet compliance standards. Organizations such as AAOIFI and IFBS are continually releasing new standards on documentation to address this problem.

Credit Risk Scoring and Modelling

Another area of Islamic finance that requires innovation is the assessment of risk associated with the creditworthiness of consumers. In the vast majority of nations with large unbanked populations, consumer credit rating agencies are non-existent and financial institutions must build credit histories and profiles on a case-by-case basis. This labour-intensive process introduces additional costs that are ultimately passed on to consumers. When these products are offered in competitive markets, the added costs make Islamic finance appear to be more costly to consumers than conventional products. However, products can be offered not only after an assessment of a customer's creditworthiness, but also by linking the customer assessment to the risks of the structure of the financial product. For example, products for low-risk customer segments can be structured on a *musharakah* basis, whereas for relatively riskier customers, finance may be extended on a *murabahah* basis. In addition, some Shariah scholars believe that *musharakah* and *murabahah* are the ideal structures and, where possible, they are to be preferred over structures such as *mudarabah*. Risk scoring and modelling tools could assist in moving customers with good credit histories from sales-based structures to partnership (*musharakah* and *mudarabah*) structures, thereby increasing the representation of partnership-based advances in the overall portfolio.

Notes

1   State of world population 2008 report, United Nations Population Division, www.unfpa.org/swp/2008/presskit/docs/en-swop08-report.pdf.

2   Shape of Things to Come interactive database, Population Action International, Washington, DC, 2007, www.populationaction.org, and Maris Strategies' estimates.

3   Taylor, J.B. (2004) Understanding and supporting Islamic finance: product differentiation and international standards, keynote address to the Harvard Islamic Finance Forum, Harvard University, May 8.

4   Y-Sing, L. and Li Lian, L. (2009) Sharia harmonisation possible in long run, Thai Bank, Arabian Business.com, March 2, www.arabianbusiness.com/.

5   Root, S. (2003) Branding for banks, *UBS News for Banks*, 4: 2.

6   Interview with Adam Wurf, co-founder of the Madano Partnership, by author, March, 2009.

7   European Islamic Investment Bank and Liquidity Management Centre sign strategic co-operation agreement, *AME Info*, December 10, 2006, www.ameinfo.com/104795.html.

8   Čihák, M. and Hesse, H. (2008) Islamic banks and financial stability: an empirical analysis, IMF Working Paper, p. 21.

9   Čihák, M. and Hesse, H. (2008) Study shows larger Islamic banks need prudential eye, IMF Survey Magazine, May 19, www.imf.org/external/pubs/ft/survey/so/2008/RES051908A.htm.

10 FRBSF Economic Letter, Federal Reserve Bank of San Francisco, no. 2002-02, January 25, 2002, www.frbsf.org.

11 Čihák, M. and Hesse, H. (2008) Islamic banks and financial stability: an empirical analysis, IMF Working Paper, pp. 21–2.

12 Growing pains: managing Islamic banking risks, PricewaterhouseCoopers, White Paper, 2008.

13 Central Bank of Bahrain, *Rulebook*, vol. 2, *Islamic Banks*, module CA-A, rule reference CA-A.3.2, March, 2005.

14 Taylor, J.B. (2004) Understanding and supporting Islamic finance: product differentiation and international standards, keynote address to the Harvard Islamic Finance Forum, Harvard University, May 8.

15 Ariff, M. (2008) What do we know of Islamic bank efficiency?, presentation at Islamic Finance Colloquium, Melbourne, Australia, 23 October, p. 16.

16 Hussein, K.A. (2004) Banking efficiency in Bahrain: Islamic vs conventional banks, Jeddah: Islamic Development Bank, Research Paper No. 68, p. 31.

17 Hussein, K.A., Banking efficiency in Bahrain: Islamic vs conventional banks, pp. 41–2.

CONCLUSION

During the course of this book, we have argued the merits of Islamic financial innovation in the context of the global economic crisis that is shaping the early years of the twenty-first century. Our intention has been to demonstrate the use of Shariah-based financial products as a viable mechanism for consumers, business and governments to finance their lifestyles, corporate activities and investments.

We have explored two questions on the future of the industry: Where does Islamic finance fit into the overall global economic framework? How is innovation in Islamic finance adapting to serve Muslim and non-Muslim communities? In the economic climate of 2009, industry pundits argue that Islamic finance may be the cure-all for the financial mistakes of laissez faire capitalism. Industry detractors argue that Islamic finance is merely an emerging fad, which has come and gone in the past. Regardless of these two extreme views, Islamic finance is demonstrating that it is a viable alternative in worldwide conventional financial markets. Whether Islamic finance is a cure to the shortcomings of capitalism is yet to be determined. The architect Buckminster Fuller once told a story that puts these diverse opinions into context:

> If a ship sinks and your find a piano top floating on the surface of the water, you can climb on board and use it as a life preserver, but this does not mean we should design life preservers that look like piano tops.

Critics of Islamic finance argue that there is a clash of cultures, which will dampen the enthusiasm for Islamic finance in Western nations. Saumitra Jha noted that there is a proportional relationship between religious/cultural tolerance and economic interdependence, suggesting that socio-political unrest reduces as the economic health of a nation improves. Put simply, when people depend on each other for economic viability, there is less unrest in society. As Saumitra Jha notes, there was economic symbiosis between Muslims and Hindus in India during much of the Middle Ages, when the cost of replicating a complementary service provided by one group to another was high and social intolerance and violence were low.[1] Saumitra Jha observed that the co-dependence within India's Muslim/Hindu society maintained social parity, until that balance was altered by an outside force, namely the British Empire during the nineteenth century. Therefore, the balance brought on by interdependence places each party in a similar operating state of shared risk/shared return, which is the fundamental tenet of Islamic finance. If history is an indicator of future human behaviour, perhaps the rise of Islamic financial innovation is a first step on the journey to a higher degree of financial and political stability.

One final point to be made about Islamic financial innovation is that there are differences between conventional and Muslim economies, which must be considered. Ideologically, there is a difference between the economic goals of laissez faire capitalism and the Islamic tenet of equality. An oversimplification of the two ideological constructs can be said as: in capitalism, there is implicit intent that the markets, customers and supplies will act in the interest of the greater good, which will, over time, balance greed, whereas in Islamic finance, the same balance is an explicit intent to find fairness and a just price. This highlights the very essence of what may be the driver of the third generation of Islamic finance innovation – the difference between "self-interest" and "the greater good". The debate over the explicit goals of Islamic economic theory bring into sharp contrast an interesting idea when thinking about the next generation of Islamic products. The implication of the debate between self-interest versus the care for others is more than a philosophical discussion, as it resonates to the very core of Islamic macroeconomics – to produce a higher GDP or achieve balanced growth with equitable distribution.[2] This parallels a similar ongoing debate in capitalist academic circles.

There is an old Arab proverb that best summarizes the state of Islamic finance in early 2009: a promise is a cloud, fulfilment is rain. In the context of Shariah-compliant banks operating in the world today, this translates into a simple message: for several years, the Islamic finance industry has been building capacity to demonstrate to Muslims and non-Muslims the inherent value of Shariah-compliant banking products and services. Currently the industry is maturing to the point where expansion of Shariah-compliant services is only limited by the ambition and imagination of a bank's senior management team. Fulfilment is accomplished by the speed at which Islamic institutions can capitalize on market opportunities.

All organizations follow a familiar pattern of growth and maturity. As an industry, Islamic finance is moving from a period of randomized and highly competition-led technological implementations to an era of applying technology to the challenges of business. This is, indeed, the heart of innovation. This is an important distinction for Shariah-compliant financial institutions operating in emerging economies, because unlike their European or North American counterparts, banks in emerging economies have fewer legacy systems to undo in order to take advantage of what today's technology has to offer. The ability of Shariah-compliant small to medium-sized financial institutions to rapidly apply and adapt technology provides them with an opportunity to leapfrog larger or better capitalized banks, giving smaller institutions in the region a strategic competitive advantage.

The technological advantage that is inherent in a smaller Islamic financial institution lies in its ability to change rapidly the product mix to accommodate a wide range of Muslim lifestyles while preserving Islamic ideals. To capitalize on this advantage, Shariah-compliant institutions must develop a strategy for top-line growth that integrates technology into three key areas of the bank:

1 leveraging the abilities of the people employed

2 using technology in new ways, to do new things, in new markets, or to engage customers, not merely to sell them products

3 rethinking the fundamentals of how an institution provides value or, perhaps more specifically, rethinking primary business processes, organizational measurements and how to engage customers.

Islamic financial institutions have a longstanding tradition of adapting technology to best serve businesses and customers of all socioeconomic classes. Perhaps a century or two before the tenth century, Arab travellers brought a new technology from the Indus Valley, which they adapted into a distinct advantage to facilitate commerce, enabling them to go beyond their European counterparts for almost two centuries. That technology was the use of the zero as a mathematical placeholder. The applied use of the zero revolutionized basic mathematics, transforming the addition, subtraction, multiplication and division of Roman numerals into a quick easy tool to facilitate the tallying and recording of financial transactions. The zero was instrumental in shaping what we call banking today, as well as how we see the world today. In tenth-century Italy, bankers learned the use of the zero from the Arabs, and decided that it was such a competitive advantage that they kept it secret from most of Europe and dominated banking, finance and trade for almost two centuries. Once the secret was out and Europeans believed they had achieved technological parity with the Middle East in the late medieval period, they were again surprised by innovations such as *sutfaya* (bills of exchange) and *mohatra* – a form of forward contract used by Arab traders of the day. Once again, it was the applied use of the zero and the sophistication of Arab financial instruments facilitated by the zero that was surprising to European banks.

Historically, the transition from Arab mathematical knowledge to applied European use took centuries. Perhaps today we stand at the dawn of yet another innovative banking shift – a financial system based on morals and ethical values, which offers an alternative to interest-bearing monetary instruments and services. Just as historical financial performance is not a clear indicator of the future performance of an institution, the factors shaping the future of banking in any given region are never certain. However, if, as the Arab proverb described, the clouds on the horizon do indeed bring rain, it will be the numerous opportunities for banks in the region to leapfrog their competitors, expand into new markets and capitalize on a host of new opportunities, all as a direct result of leveraging their organizations with technology. However, in the long term, the nature of global competition will become more evident for Islamic finance, because although today we are basking in the media limelight, this same light brings the spotlight of international scrutiny. Shariah-compliant banks will not only have to face competition from big players, they will also be subject to increased regulatory examination from international sources and security organizations.

What we have observed during the research for this book is that many practioners of Islamic finance are concerned with social issues as well as profit. Unlike conventional bankers, whose social concerns are often the product of a corporate social responsibility agenda, the majority of Shariah-compliant bankers we interviewed held a fundamental belief that the role of the financial institution is to ensure the values of Islamic finance such as equality and fair play. The preservation of these ideals was paramount in their thinking versus the loss of a few fees or a reduced return on investment. This is not to say that Shariah-compliant bankers are not concerned with generating a profit. The overarching sentiment from bankers was that their concerns centred on generating a socially responsible profit. The result is that the value proposition of Shariah-compliant institutions is often increased in the communities they serve, fostering higher levels of customer loyalty and a greater sense of integrated social responsibility. To put this into a global perspective, while conventional banks exercise their social responsibilities by simply giving money to charities, Islamic finance actively helps people to escape poverty, start businesses, finance development projects and take banking beyond the threshold of traditional banking services. Indeed, the ethical acumen of Islamic finance stands in sharp contrast to the values of western banking.

As the Islamic finance industry continues on its journey of market maturity, the key to the next generation of the industry will be to achieve top-line growth through innovation and capitalizing on what we can learn from each other, as Shariah-compliant banks. In most markets today, our focus is to develop competitive strategies to bring more Muslims from informal to formal economic systems. Our mandate as bankers is to take what has been learned during the first generation of Islamic finance and apply it in innovative ways to facilitate the lifestyles of Muslim and non-Muslim customers and assist them in achieving their economic goals. This brings to mind another Arab proverb: knowledge without practice or application is a tree without fruit. At this stage of market development in Islamic finance, the time has come to harvest the fruit, capitalize on our technology investments, reinforce Islamic ethical and moral ideals, and use the next generation of products to engage our customers, partners, communities and nations in a new era of economic growth.

Notes

1 Jha, S. (2008) Trade, institutions and religious tolerance: evidence from India, Stanford University, Research Paper no. 2004, January, pp. 7–11.

2 Khan, M.F., Islamic science of economics: to be or not to be, Islamic Society of Institutional Economics, www.i-sie.org.

GLOSSARY

AAOIFI (Accounting and Auditing Organization for Islamic Financial Institutions) – Established in 1991 in Bahrain, the AAOIFI is an Islamic international, autonomous and non-profit-making corporate body that prepares accounting, auditing, governance, ethics and Shariah standards for Islamic financial institutions.

al-ijarah thumma al bai **(hire purchase)** – There are two contracts involved in this concept. The first contract is called *ijarah* (see below) and the second contract is based on *bai* (see below); these two contracts are undertaken one after the other. For example, in a vehicle financing facility, a customer enters into the first contract and leases the car from the owner (bank) at an agreed rental over a determined period. When the leasing period expires, the second contract comes into effect, which enables the customer to purchase the car at an agreed price. This type of transaction is particularly reminiscent of *contractum trinius*, a complicated legal instrument used by European bankers and merchants during the Middle Ages, which involved combining three legal contracts in order to produce a transaction of a hidden interest-bearing loan (something that the Church made illegal). The *al-ijarah thumma al bai*, however, does not carry interest.

bai – Contract for purchase.

bai al-dayn **(debt trading)** – Refers to debt financing, that is, the provision of financial resources that are required for production, commerce and services through the sale and/or purchase of trade documents and papers. It is a short-term facility with a maturity of not more than a year. Only documents evidencing real debts arising from bona fide commercial transactions can be traded.

bai al-inah **(sell and buy back agreement)** – If a loan is needed, a financier sells an asset to the customer on a deferred payment, and then the asset is immediately repurchased by the borrower for cash at a discount, so that the borrower has extra cash in the transaction. The buying back agreement allows the bank to assume ownership over the asset in order to protect against default without explicitly charging interest in the event of late payments or insolvency.

bai al-istijrar (**supply contract**) – This form of contract refers to an agreement between the client and the supplier whereby the supplier agrees to provide a particular product on an ongoing basis and at an agreed price on the basis of an agreed mode of payment.

bai al-salam, bay-salaam **or** *salam* (**future delivery**) – One of the basic conditions for the validity of a sale in Shariah law is that the commodity intended to be sold must be in the physical or constructive possession of the seller. This condition has three implications: first, the commodity must exist (advance payment is problematic, as something which does not exist cannot be sold); second, the seller should have acquired the ownership of that commodity in order to sell it; and third, ownership in paper is not sufficient. The commodity should have come in the possession of the seller, either physically or constructively. *Salam* and *istisna* are two special exceptions to Shariah. *Bai al-salam* is a sale whereby the seller undertakes to supply some specific goods to the buyer at a future date in exchange for an advanced price fully paid on the spot. It refers to an agreement whereby payment is made immediately while the goods are delivered at a later date. It is equivalent to an advance payment or retainer.

bai bithaman ajil (**deferred payment sale**) – Typical of Malaysia and some other Southeast Asian countries, it is a form of *murabahah* in which payment is made in instalments some time after delivery of goods. This form of sale is based on the selling of goods on a deferred payment basis at a price, which includes a profit margin agreed by both parties. It is similar to *murabahah* (see below), except that the debtor makes only a single instalment on the maturity date of the loan rather than on a regular basis.

gharar – Uncertainty. With *riba* (interest) and *maysir* (gambling), the three forbidden elements of Islamic finance. The prohibition of *gharar* is based on certain aspects of financial transactions such as chance or risk.

hajj – The Islamic pilgrimage to Mecca.

halal – Arabic-speaking countries use *halal* to describe anything that is permissible under Islamic law. Non-Arabic-speaking countries generally use *halal* in a narrower context of Muslim dietary laws.

haram **or** *haraam* – Something that is forbidden by Islam, and indeed anything that is prohibited by the faith.

hawala **or** *hiwalah* (**remittance**) – Refers to a transfer of funds/debt from the depositor's/ debtor's account to the receiver's/creditor's account where a commission may be charged for such service.

ijarah (**leasing**) – A medium-term mode of financing referring to an arrangement under which the lessor leases equipment, a building or other facility to a client at an agreed rental against a fixed charge, as agreed by both parties. It involves purchasing and subsequently transferring the right of use of the equipment and machinery to the beneficiary for a specific period of time.

IRTI (Islamic Research and Training Institute) – Established in 1981 to undertake research, training and information activities on Islamic economic, financial and banking issues.

mudarabah, mudaraba, mudharabah or *modaraba* (**profit sharing**) – The term *mudarabah* is Arabic and implies an investment partnership contract, whereby the investor (the *rab ul mal*) entrusts money to the other party/entrepreneur (the *mudarib*) in order to undertake a business/investment activity. Profits of the *mudarabah* are shared in a pre-agreed ratio and losses in the proportion of the capital invested. Losses are borne by the investor (*mudarib*) only.

mudarabah **agreement** – A set of legal agreements signed between the parties to a syndicated financing, usually includes a financing agreement.

mudarib – A contracting party in a *mudarabah* financing, who acts in a fiduciary capacity as the agent or fund manager.

murabahah or *murabaha* (**purchase and resale**) – A sales contract between a buyer and a seller, whereby the selling price is based on costs plus a profit margin that is clearly stated to the buyer at the time of the agreement. In some cases, the payment for the purchase consists of instalment payments specified in the initial sale agreement. Instead of lending out money, the capital provider purchases the commodity for which the loan would have been taken out from an independent third party and resells it to the person interested at a predetermined higher price to the capital user. By paying this higher price over instalments, the capital user has effectively obtained credit without paying interest. This type of transaction is similar to "rent-to-own" arrangements for furniture or appliances that are common in US stores. *Murabahah* is one of the most common types of mortgage-like agreements in Islamic banking.

musharakah or *musyarakah* (**joint venture or profit and loss sharing**) – Refers to a partnership or joint venture for a specific business with a profit motive, whereby the distribution of profits will be apportioned as per the investment of each partner and according to an agreed ratio. In the event of losses, both parties will share the losses based on their equity participation. It is similar to a conventional partnership structure as well as the ownership of voting stock in a limited company. This equity financing arrangement is widely regarded as the purest form of Islamic financing as it is based on sharing risk and profits. It also appears as *mutanaqisa* (or diminishing/declining participation). There are many subdivisions of the concept, including *sharikah al milk* (partnership based on joint ownership, which may be voluntary, for example in the purchase of an item, or involuntary, as in the case of inheritance), *sharikah al uqud* (partnership based on a contractual relationship) and others.

riba (interest) – Any return of money made on lending money whether the interest is fixed or not, simple or compounded, and at whatever rate. *Riba* is prohibited under Islamic law.

Shariah, Sharia, Shari'ah, Shari'a, Sharia'a – Islamic law, governing the life of Muslims, which is derived from the Holy Qur'an and Sunnah. Shariah-compliant products and services meet the requirements of Islamic law and are allowed.

Shariah advisory council/consultant – Islamic banks and banking institutions that offer Islamic banking products and services (IBS banks) are required to establish Shariah advisory committees/consultants to advise them and to ensure that the operations and activities of the bank comply with Shariah principles. In Malaysia, the National Shariah Advisory Council advises Bank Negara Malaysia on the Shariah aspects of its operations, as well as on its products and services.

Shariah committee – An independent body comprising specialized jurists in *fiqh almua malat* (Islamic commercial jurisprudence) responsible for directing, reviewing and supervising the activities of the Islamic financial institution to ensure that it complies with Shariah rules and principles.

sukuk – Similar to a conventional bond, with the difference of being asset backed to comply with the no *gharar* rule. A *sukuk* represents proportionate beneficial ownership in the underlying asset. The asset will be leased to the client to yield the return on the *sukuk*.

takaful – Islamic insurance. It is characterized by a charitable collective pool of funds based on the idea of mutual assistance. This form of insurance is designed to avoid the elements of conventional insurance (interest and gambling) that are forbidden for Muslims.

tawarruq – Reverse *murabahah*. As used in personal financing, a customer with a genuine need purchases goods on credit from the bank on a deferred payment basis and then immediately resells it for cash to a third party in order to obtain cash. In this way, the customer can obtain cash without taking an interest-based loan.

ujr (fee) – Refers to commissions or fees charged for services.

wakalah (agency) – When a person appoints a representative to undertake transactions on their behalf. It is the equivalent to a power of attorney.

waqf – An endowment or a charitable trust devoted exclusively for Islamic purposes.

Waqf Fund – A trust fund set up in Islamic year 1399H (1979) for financing special assistance operations, scholarship programmes, technical cooperation programmes, the Islamic Research and Training Institute (IRTI), technical assistance, LDMCs Special Account, and the Adahi Sacrificial Meat Utilization Project.

zakat – A religious levy ordained on Muslims and payable annually at a rate of 2.5% net assets to certain beneficiaries prescribed by Shariah.

BIBLIOGRAPHY

Ariff, M. (1988) Islamic banking, *Asian-Pacific Economic Literature*, **2**(2): 48–64.

Barucci, P. (1985) A letter of credit drawn on the past, *UNESCO Courier*, February.

Brandenburger, A. and Nalebuff, B. (1996) *Co-Opetition: A Revolution Mindset that Combines Competition and Cooperation*, New York, Bantam Doubleday Dell.

Brotton, J. (2003) *The Renaissance Bazaar: From the Silk Road to Michelangelo*, Oxford University Press.

Bursa Malaysia (2008) Innovation: driving the future of Malaysia's Islamic capital market, *Islamic Finance Asia*, August/September.

Čihák, M. and Hesse, H. (2008) Islamic banks and financial stability: an empirical analysis, IMF Working Paper, WP/08/06.

Creutz, H. (2001) *Das Geld Syndrom: Wege zu einer krisenfreien Marktwirtschaft*, Broschiert.

DiVanna, J. (2006) *Understanding Islamic Banking*, Cambridge, Leonardo and Francis Press.

DiVanna, J. (2007) Top 500 Islamic finance institutions, *The Banker*, November.

DiVanna, J. (2008) Top 500 Islamic finance institutions, *The Banker*, November.

DiVanna, J. (2008) A cloud is a promise, fulfilment is rain, *New Horizon*, January–March, 167.

Encyclopaedia Britannica, 1911, Bill of exchange.

Farooq, M.O. (2006) Partnership, equity-financing and Islamic finance: whither profit-loss-sharing', Upper Iowa University, working paper, August.

Fisher, I. (1933) *Stamp Script*, New York, Adelphi.

Gesell, S. (1929) *The Natural Economic Order*, Berlin, Neo-Verlag.

Haron, S. and Wan Azmi, Wan Nursofiza (2006) Marketing strategy of Islamic banks: a lesson from Malaysia, working paper series 006, *Journal of Islamic Banking and Finance*, January–March.

Henry, P.B. (2003) Commentary on Bekaert, Harvey and Lundblad's "Equity market liberalization in emerging equity markets", Stanford University, Research Paper No. 1783, February.

Hesse, H., Jobst, A. and Sole, J. (2008) Current trends in Islamic structured finance and capital markets', IMF, September 2.

Hunt, E.S. and Murray, J.M. (1999) *A History of Business in Medieval Europe 1200–1550*, Cambridge University Press.

Hussein, K.A. (2004) Banking efficiency in Bahrain: Islamic vs conventional banks, Islamic Development Institute, Research Paper 68.

International Herald Tribune (2008) Booming Islamic bond market embroiled in debate over religious compliance, January 11.

Jha, S. (2008) Trade, institutions and religious tolerance: evidence from India, Stanford University, Research Paper 2004, January.

Jobst, A., Kunzel, P., Mills, P. and Sy, A. (2008) Islamic bond issuance: what sovereign debt managers need to know, IMF Policy Discussion Paper (PDP/08/03), July.

Karim, N., Tarazi, M. and Reille, X. (2008) Islamic microfinance: an emerging market niche, CGAP, Focus Note Number 49, August.

Kennedy, M. (2004) Local currencies in the 21st century, paper presented at Bard College, New York, June 25–27.

Keynes, J.M. (1936) *The General Theory of Employment, Interest and Money*, Basingstoke, Macmillan.

Khan, W.M. (1989) Towards an interest-free Islamic economic system, *Journal of King Abdulaziz University Islamic Economics*, vol. 1.

Lloyds Banking Company Ltd, *Rules for Branch Managers*, December, 1874.

PricewaterhouseCoopers (2008) Growing pains: managing Islamic banking risks, White Paper.

Rosly, S.A. and Abu Bakar, Mohd Afandi (2003) Performance of Islamic and mainstream banks in Malaysia, *International Journal of Social Economics*, **30**(12): 1249–65.

Schoon, N. (2007) Islamic finance: expansion brings challenges, *Professional Investor*, February.

Shigehisa, K. (2002) The enigma of "time is money", *Japan Review*, **14**: 227.

Solé, J. (2007) Introducing Islamic banking into conventional banking systems, IMF Working Paper, WP/07/175, July.

Taing, A. (2009) Can Maybank digest another acquisition?, Malaysia, *The Edge*, February 23.

Toutounchian, I. (2009) *Islamic Money and Banking: Integrating Money in Capital Theory*, Singapore, John Wiley & Sons.

Usmani, M.I.A. (2007) *A Guide to Islamic Banking (Gulf African Bank)*, Karachi, Darul Ishaat.

Vallely, P. (2006) How Islamic inventors changed the world, *The Independent* (London), March 11.

INDEX

Banks, institutions and organizations

Words and concepts